And now I know this mystery, that wrong-doers will twist and pervert the words of right doing in many ways, and will speak wicked words, and lie and practice great deceits, and write books concerning *their* words.

But when those write down truthfully all *my* words in their languages, and do not change or take away anything from my words but write them all down truthfully, all that I first testified concerning them, then I know another mystery that books will be given to the right-doers and the wise to become a cause of joy and uprightness and much wisdom. To them will the books be given. And they will believe in them and rejoice over them. Then will all the right-doers, who have learned from them all the paths of uprightness, be rewarded.

From Enoch 104

Also by
Dr. Timothy J. Sakach, Ph. D.

Prophecy Unsealed!
The Great Destiny of Human Kind
as Prophesied by the Scriptures or
How to Prepare for the Coming New Age

ENOCH

The Book Behind the Bible

or

The Great Destiny of Human Kind
Revealed to Our Father Enoch

A Revised and Edited Version
based on the Translation of 1912 by R. H. Charles

Dr. Timothy J. Sakach, Ph. D.

Innertech Publishing
Laguna Niguel, California

Published by Innertech Publishing
PO Box 7560, Laguna Niguel, California 92607

Web Site: ElahimConnection.com

"Prepare the way ... " Blog Site: Innertech.com

Keywords: History, Prophecy, Revelation, Spiritual, Scriptures, Prophets, End Age, Resurrection, Enoch, Daniel, Weeks, Righteous, Elect, Messengers. End Time

ISBN: 0-934917-05-1
EAN: 9780934917056
Ver: 1.0

Manufactured in the United States of America

Contents

Introduction

Robert H. Charles wrote a very long and, some might say, speculative, introduction to his translation of Enoch's and Noah's writings in Oxford's *Pseudepigrapha*. Charles' attempt to discredit both of these writers is obvious. His claim is that this document was written about 200 B.C. by a group of writers or scribes, *pretending* to be Enoch or Noah. However, it is nearly impossible to support such ideas because that would force us to conclude that all the other books of the Hebrew Scriptures would have been written on or about the same time. And if we can believe IV Ezra, they at least were *restored* by scribes after the return from exile.

The other conclusion, which most scholars seem to miss, is that these writings had to have been *copied* from earlier manuscripts to be preserved. That these writers or "scribes" may have included their own *comments* or "*corrections*" is not in question. Those who copied the Torah and the rest of the Hebrew Scriptures did that in many places.

However, the writings of Enoch were preserved by Noah and his sons, and known by Abraham, Isaac,and Jacob and his twelve sons, and quoted by Moses, the Prophets, and the Apostles.

I wrote in my blog, "Prepare the way ... " at

http://Innertech.com

about the importance of spiritual discernment and about the two forms of knowledge, called "lower and higher" by the sages. Charles' Introduction uses the classic form of scholarship and is a good example of what is meant by "lower knowledge."

But to make the revision of this translation, I had to call upon the power of "higher knowledge" or "spiritual discernment" to edit Charles' work and make this translation clear and plain, because without that we could only rely on the works of scholars whose desire is often to make the spiritual sound foolish, and make themselves sound intelligent. Do not get me wrong. Many great things came from the research and study in the realm of "lower knowledge," didn't they? But even greater understanding comes from the power inherent in "higher knowledge." All things in life can and should be spiritually understood, including these documents.

ABOUT THE EDITS

I replaced all King James English from this translation. Only a very small fringe speak using words like "thee" and "thou" and "ye" and "hast." Some religious leaders use these words to *sound religious*, mostly when praying. This affected speech only shows that those so afflicted are still caught up in the religious systems of this world. There is nothing spiritual about Old English, is there?

Charles used words that are now deemed archaic and obsolete. To help us see the meaning of the words, I replaced these with modern synonyms choosing the simpler, common word over the old multi-syllable one.

The word "and" appears in Charles' translation much too often. It adds little to the sense of the phrase and often destroys the meaning. I removed much of this redundancy to help make the writing more smooth on the ear. Even if the original language contained a prolific use of conjunctions, we simply don't talk that way.

Punctuation was often awkward and confusing. The frequent use of the colon [:] did not make things clearer to our eyes. So in most cases it was removed or replaced by the comma or period.

The chapter and verse numbers appeared to be arbitrary and misplaced. In some places paragraphs are verses, and in other chapters each sentence is a verse. There are also places where a verse starts in the middle of a sentence! So I superscripted verse numbers (^{1}, ^{2}, ^{3}) to help keep the sense of the paragraphs because larger size numbers break the flow.

Also experience shows that parsing Scriptures by the addition of numbered verses caused many to create contexts that were never intended. I preserved the chapter numbers as given in the original translation. But even here, in a few places, the following chapter is a continuation of the sentence or paragraph of the previous chapter! This leads me to suspect that the translator did not have a clear picture of what he was translating.

I have taught and made reference to Enoch since I first found the publication more than 30 years ago. But the task of analyzing the text, word by word, made it clear to me that this is one coherent work with only a few "speed bumps." What might have appeared confusing and difficult became clear. Now the truth shines and the power of Enoch is evident.

No other document has had such profound effect on the rest of Scriptures. When the words of Enoch are known and understood, one can sense their influence on the other writers, including Moses, the prophets, and the apostles. Enoch established the context within which all who loved the truth must write. His writings contain powerful, hope-filled messages that were intended for us to see and hear from the very beginning.

Enoch is also quoted in the *The Book of Jasher*, *Testament of the Twelve Patriarchs*, the *Book of Jubilees*, and by Peter and Jude (*New Testament*) who reckoned it as Scripture written by Enoch. Enoch forms an unquestionable context from which both the prophets and apostles wrote. So strong is the influence of Enoch on their thoughts that neither the Hebrew Scriptures or the New Testament could have been written without Enoch. Moses, the prophets, and the apostles did not question the authority or inspiration of Enoch. Should we?

After reading and understanding, the righteous, according to Enoch, will recognize his writings to be both revelation and inspiration, the product of advanced theology and prophecy that transcends time and prevailing opinions.

Enoch is the mysterious righteous father of us all and the scribe who wrote "The Book Behind the Bible!"

The Book of the Watchers

T he first book of Enoch is also called the Book of the Watchers. It talks about an earth unknown to us because of its simplicity. Enoch writes about the difference between the seasons, of trees that shed their leaves, except for fourteen types. He ponders the moon, the sun and the stars, and creates a picture of a time when the creation was still in its childhood phase. The genetic material, though rich in its potential, had only begun to give birth to creatures, insects, plant life, and various forms of human life.

Recently, it has come to the attention of science that the Neanderthals lived side-by-side with other forms of human life. They could speak and be understood, according to the research. However, it would not be surprising if Neanderthals also shared the same mitochondria with others who we, in our *wisdom*, would have considered more "normal" human beings.

During this time it was not unusual for beings from the Domain of Elohim to visit and communicate with humanity. These were called the "Watchers" in Enoch's writing. We would call them "angels" today. But these were really Messengers sent to help those who would inherit salvation. However, as the population of the earth increased so also did the problems.

Led by a Watcher by the name of Samjaza, other Messengers found that the daughters of Mankind were beautiful and alluring. And they wanted to take wives to themselves and have children by them. To do this they made for themselves bodies that in their twisted way of thinking were well endowed with penises like those of horses. One account says that they took the form of the husbands. By sexually uniting with the women, the Watchers "sinned" or "committed a big error," and caused the women to conceive and give birth to both sons and daughters. There is only a brief reference to this in the book of Genesis, where it is written that they gave birth to giants, or at least to men of great stature: "three hundred cubits." However, they also gave birth to women who were even more attractive than human women. In other words, they pushed the limits on both the male and female genetics, and these became a product of both physical and spiritual forces. But in doing this, these Messengers, the Watchers, missed the goal that was set before humanity and instead deceived and corrupted the human race!

From this tragedy has proceeded all the stories of giants that we love to teach our children: Jack and the Bean Stalk, the dragon slayers, and even the ogre Shrek! And not only that but also the Sirens of the Odysseus, witchcraft, spiritism, and prostitution also came from these.

Enoch records who was responsible for these problems and what will become of them. He wrote how these offspring of spiritual and physical powers became the demons and sirens of the earth. These would continue to plague humankind until the time of the their judgment and sentencing.

But the great error of the Watchers did not stop with sex. They also taught the use of makeup or face painting, charms, astrology, the use of contracts in place of righteousness, how to build weapons, and how to kill, how to make drugs or potions from plants, and many other things that humans in their innocence could have survived without.

This came about under the leadership of another Watcher named Azazel. Upon his head has been placed all of the deception that has turned humankind from the precious relation with their Creator into inter-personal *relationships* based upon doing wrong, and following partial and corrupt knowledge.

Azazel is the Hebrew word in Leviticus 16 concerning one of the two goats used in the Day of Atonement (or Yom KPR). One goat was set apart for Eyahuwah and was sacrificed, "because of the uncleanness of the children of Israel, and because of their violations caused by all their errors and mistakes."

The other goat was set-apart for "Azazel:"

But the goat on which the lot for Azazel fell is caused
to stand alive before Eyahuwah, to make *atonement* upon

ENOCH: THE BOOK BEHIND THE BIBLE

it, to send it into the wilderness to Azazel ... Then Aaron shall lay both his hands on the head of the live goat, and shall confess over it all the crookedness of the children of Israel, and all their violations caused by their errors and mistakes, and shall put them on the head of the goat, and shall send it away into the wilderness by the hand of a fit man. And the goat shall bear on itself all their crookedness, to a land cut off. Thus, he shall send the goat away into the wilderness.

Why send this goat away after confessing over it the errors, mistakes, and crookedness of the People? Because Azazel, the Watcher who led the people astray was taken to a set place on earth to be kept incarcerated until the time of judgment. This is the meaning of the service of the Day of Atonement. Yet few now even know that Messengers under the leadership of Azazel are held *accountable* for the problems and crookedness that brings all the suffering and trouble upon human kind even to this day. Instead we get "cute" and call it the day of "At – one – ment." What this High Day really tell us is that the sin must be placed on the head of another, and that this crookedness and massive error is "not our fault." It is the fault of the one who brought it to earth in the first place.

It is this understanding that makes Enoch's Book of the Watchers so very important to our spiritual well-being and life. The Hebrew word translated "atonement" is כפר or in Ancient Hebrew ꟼ⌒ש or KPR which means to "cover as with a lid" (Aaron's two hands on the head of the goat for Azazel.) By "putting a lid on it" and sending if off to Azazel in the wilderness shows that the crookedness and wrong-doing is the fault of the Watchers who went astray, not to the people who suffer because of it.

Yom Kippur is the "Day of Covering." The "Day of Atonement" came to be in the 16th Century. Enoch recorded the true story in "The Book of the Watchers," and here it is ...

THE BOOK OF THE WATCHERS

CHAPTER 1
The words of the blessing of Enoch, wherewith he blessed the elect

[chosen] and those who do what is right, who will be living in the day of tribulation, when all the wicked and godless are to be removed.

²And Enoch, a right-doing man whose eyes were opened by Elah, saw the vision of the Holy One in the heavens, took up his parable and said,

"The Messengers showed me. From them I heard everything, and from them I understood as I saw, but not for this generation, but for a remote one which is to come.

³"Concerning the elect I took up my parable concerning them, and said:

"The Set-apart Great One will come from His dwelling. ⁴The eternal Elohim will tread upon the earth, [even on Mount Sinai,] and appear from His camp in the strength of His might from the heaven of heavens.

⁵"And all will be struck with fear, and the Watchers will quake. Great fear and trembling will seize them. ⁶To the ends of the earth the high mountains will be shaken, and the high hills will be made low, and melt like wax before the flame. ⁷The earth will be wholly torn apart, and all living things upon the earth will die. A judgment will be upon all.

⁸"But with the right-doers He will make peace and will protect the chosen, and mercy will be on them. And they will all belong to Elah, and they will be prospered, and they will all be blessed. He will help them all. And light will appear to them, and He will make peace with them.

⁹"And look! He comes with ten thousands of His set-apart ones to execute judgment on all, and to destroy all the ungodly, and to convict all flesh of all the works of their ungodliness that they have ungodly committed, and of all the hard things that ungodly sinners have spoken against Him."

CHAPTER 2

Observe everything that takes place in the heaven. Note how they do not change their orbits. And see the luminaries, which are in the heaven, how they all rise and set in order, each in its season. They do not transgress against their appointed order.

²Look at the earth, and pay attention to the things that take place upon it from first to last. See how steadfast they are and how none of the things on earth change, but all the works of Elah are evident to you. ³Observe the summer and the winter, how the whole earth is filled with water, and clouds, dew, and rain lie upon it.

CHAPTER 3

Observe and see how in the winter all the trees seem as though they had withered and shed all their leaves, except fourteen trees, which do not lose their foliage but retain the old foliage from two to three years till the new comes.

CHAPTER 4

And again, observe the days of summer how the sun is above the earth and high overhead. And you seek shade and shelter because of the heat of the sun. The earth also burns with growing heat, and you cannot walk barefoot on the earth or on a rock because of the heat.

CHAPTER 5

Observe how the trees cover themselves with green leaves and bear fruit. Pay attention to this and know with regard to all His works, and recognize how He that lives forever has made them this way. ²And all His works go on from year after year forever. All the tasks that they accomplish for Him do not change, but accordingly, as Elah has appointed, so is it done. ³And look how the sea and the rivers in like manner accomplish and do not change their tasks from His commandments.

⁴But you have not been resolute. Nor have you fully carried out the commandments of the Lord. Rather, you have turned away and spoken proud and hard words out of your impure mouths against His greatness. Oh, you hard-hearted, you will find no peace. ⁵You will curse your days, and the years of your life shall be ruined, and the years of your destruction will be multiplied in eternal curses. You will find no mercy. ⁶In those days you will make your names an everlasting curse to all the right-doers. By you will all

who curse, curse. All the doers of wrong and the godless shall make curses by you. [7]For you, the godless, there shall be a curse. And for all of you sinners there shall be no salvation, but on you all shall abide a curse.

All the [right-doers] will rejoice. There will be forgiveness of gross errors and serious mistakes, and every mercy, peace, and leniency. There will be salvation to them, a considerable light.

For the chosen [as distinct from the right-doers] there will be light, joy, and peace. They will inherit the earth. [8]And then there will be bestowed upon the chosen wisdom, and they will all live and never again make gross errors and serious mistakes, either through ungodliness or through pride.

But they who are wise shall be humble, [9]and they shall not again transgress, nor will they make gross and serious errors all the days of their life. Nor will they die of the divine anger or wrath. They will complete the number of the days of their life, and their lives will be increased in peace, and the years of their joy will be multiplied in eternal gladness and peace all the days of their life.

CHAPTER 6

It came to pass when the children of men had multiplied that in those days were born to them beautiful daughters of pleasing appearance. [2]And the Messengers, the children of the heaven, saw and lusted after them, and said to one another: "Come, let us choose wives from among the children of men and have children by them."

[3]Semjaza, their leader, said to the Messengers:

> "I fear you will not indeed agree to do this deed, and I
> alone shall have to pay the penalty of a great error."

[4]And they all answered him and said:

> "Let us all swear an oath, and all bind ourselves by
> mutually invoking a curse to not abandon this plan but to
> do this thing."

[5]Then they all swore together and bound themselves by mutually invoking a curse. [6]There were two hundred; who descended in the days of Jared on the summit of Mount Hermon, and they called it Mount Hermon, because they had sworn and bound themselves by mutually invoking a curse.

⁷These are the names of their leaders: Samlazaz, their leader, Araklba, Rameel, Kokablel, Tamlel, Ramlel, Danel, Ezeqeel, Baraqijal, Asael, Armaros, Batarel, Ananel, Zaq1el, Samsapeel, Satarel, Turel, Jomjael, Sariel. ⁸These are their chiefs of tens.

CHAPTER 7

All the others with their leaders took wives, and each chose one for himself, and they went in to them to defile themselves with them. And they taught their wives charms and enchantments, and the cutting of roots, and made them acquainted with plants. ²And [the wives] became pregnant, and they gave birth to great giants, whose height was **three hundred cubits.**ᵃ ³These took all the property, food, and possessions of Mankind. And when Mankind could no longer sustain them, ⁴the giants turned against them and cannibalized Mankind. ⁵And the giants began to sin against birds, beasts, reptiles, and fish. And they begin to devour each other's flesh and drink the blood. ⁶Then the earth laid accusation against these lawless ones.

a: A cubit is the length of the arm from the tip of the middle finger to the elbow – an 'ell'.

CHAPTER 8

Azazel taught Mankind to make swords, knives, shields, and breastplates, and he made known to them the metals of the earth, the art of working them into bracelets and ornaments, the use of antimony, the beautifying of the eyelids, all kinds of costly stones, and all coloring dyes. ³Semjaza taught enchantments, and root-cuttings; Armaros, the resolving of enchantments; Baraqijal astrology; Kokabel the constellations; Ezeqeel the knowledge of the clouds; Araqiel the signs of the earth; Shamsiel the signs of the sun; and Sariel the course of the moon.

²There arose much godlessness among Mankind. They committed fornication. They were led astray and became corrupt in all their ways. ⁴And as Mankind began to perish, they cried, and their cry went up to heaven.

CHAPTER 9

Then Michael, Uriel, Raphael, and Gabriel looked down from heaven and saw much blood being spilled upon the earth, and all lawlessness being produced upon the earth. ²And they talked together and said:

"The earth, made without inhabitant, now cries, and
the voice of their crying reaches to the gates of heaven.
³And now to you, the set-apart ones of heaven, the souls
of Mankind make their suit, saying, 'Bring our cause before the Most High.' "

⁴And they said to the Lord of the ages:

"Lord of lords, God of gods, King of kings, and God of
the ages, the throne of Your glory endures to all the generations of the ages, and Your name is set-apart, glorious,
and blessed for all the ages! ⁵You made all things, and
You have power over all things. And all things are naked
and open in Your sight. You see all things, and nothing
can hide itself from You. ⁶You see what Azazel has done,
how he has taught all wrong doing on earth and revealed
the eternal secrets that were preserved in heaven, which
Mankind was striving to learn. ⁷And [you see] Semjaza, to
whom You gave authority to bear rule over his associates.

⁸"They have gone to the daughters of Mankind upon
the earth, slept with the women, defiled themselves, and
revealed to them all kinds of wrong ways. ⁹These women
gave birth to giants, and the giants filled the whole earth
with blood and wrong doing.

¹⁰"Now, look at this: the souls of those who have died
are crying and making their suit to the gates of heaven,
and their woeful crying ascended and cannot cease because of the lawless deeds that are produced on the earth.
¹¹You know all things before they come to pass, and You
see these things. Yet You allow them! And You do not say
to us what we are to do to them in regard to these."

CHAPTER 10

Then the Most High, the Separate and Great One spoke and sent Uriel to
the son of Lamech, and said to him:

²"Go to Noah and tell him in My Name 'Hide yourself!'

Reveal to him the end that is approaching, that the whole earth will be destroyed, and a deluge is about to come upon the whole earth to destroy all that is on it. ³Instruct him that he may escape and his seed may be preserved for all the generations of the world."

⁴And again the Lord said to Raphael:

"Bind Azazel hand and foot, cast him into the darkness, and make an opening in the desert, which is in Dudael, and cast him there. ⁵Place upon him rough and jagged rocks, cover [KPR] him with darkness. Let him abide there forever [the ages], and cover his face that he will not see light. ⁶And on the day of the great judgment he will be cast into the fire. ⁷Heal the earth that the Messengers corrupted, and proclaim the healing of the earth that they may heal the plague, and that all the children of men may not perish through all the secret things that the Watchers disclosed and taught their sons. ⁸The whole earth has been corrupted through the works taught by Azazel. To him ascribe all sin [corruption, and wrong doing]."

⁹And to Gabriel said the Lord:

"Proceed against the bastards and the reprobates, and against the children of fornication, and destroy the children of the Watchers from among Mankind. Send them one against the other that they may destroy each other in battle. A long life they will not have. ¹⁰And no request that their fathers make of you will be granted to their fathers on their behalf. For they hope to live an eternal life and that each one of them will live five hundred years."

¹¹And the Lord said unto Michael:

"Go bind Semjaza and his associates who have united themselves with women so as to have defiled themselves with them in all their uncleanness. ¹²And when their sons have slain each other, and they have seen the destruction of their beloved ones, bind them fast for seventy generations in the valleys of the earth until the day of their judgment and ultimate end, until the judgment that is forever and ever is finished. [13]In those days they shall be led off to the abyss of fire, to the torment and the prison in which they shall be confined forever. [14]And who ever will be condemned and destroyed will from that time forward be bound together with them to the end of all generations. [15]And destroy all the spirits of the reprobate and the children of the Watchers, because they have wronged Mankind. [16]Destroy all wrong from the face of the earth and let every evil work come to an end.

"Let the plant of doing right and truth appear, and it will prove a blessing. The works of doing right and truth will be planted in truth and joy forever. [17]And then will all the right-doers escape and live until they beget thousands of children. And all the days of their youth and their old age will they complete in peace. [18]And then shall the whole earth be plowed in righteousness, be planted with trees, and be full of blessing. [19]And all desirable trees shall be planted on it. They shall plant vines on it and the vines that they plant will yield wine in abundance. As for all the seed sown on the earth, each measure will bear a thousand. And each measure of olives shall yield ten presses of oil. [20]And cleanse the earth from all oppression, from all wrong doing, from all error, and from all godlessness. All the uncleanness that is produced upon the earth, destroy from off the earth.

[21]"And all the children of men will become right-doers, and all nations will offer adoration and will praise Me, and all will worship Me. [22]And the earth will be cleansed from all defilement, from all the mistakes and errors, from all punishment, and from all torment, and I shall never again send [this] upon it from generation to generation and forever.

CHAPTER 11

"And in those days I will open the store chambers of blessing that are in heaven, to send them down upon the earth over the work and labor of the children of men. ²And truth and peace shall be associated together throughout all the days of the world and throughout all the generations of men."

CHAPTER 12

Before these things Enoch was hidden, and no one of the children of men knew where he was hidden, where he lived, and what had become of him. ²And his activities had to do with the Watchers, and his days were with the set-apart and separated ones.

³And I, Enoch, was blessing the Lord of majesty and the King of the ages, and then the Watchers called me, Enoch the writer, and said to me,

⁴"Enoch, you writer of righteousness, go, tell the Watchers of heaven who left the high heaven, the set-apart and separate eternal place, and defiled themselves with women, and did as the children of earth do, and took to themselves wives, 'You have produced great destruction on the earth, ⁵and you will have no peace or forgiveness of these gross errors. And even though you delight yourselves in your children, ⁶the murder of your beloved ones you will see, and over the destruction of your children you will lament, and make supplication unto eternity. But mercy and peace you will not attain.' "

CHAPTER 13

And Enoch went and said,

"Azazel, you will have no peace. A severe sentence has gone against you to put you in bonds. ²You will not have leniency or any request granted to you, because of the wrong knowledge that you taught, and because of all the works of godlessness, wrong-doing, and wrong ways that you have shown to Mankind."

³Then I went and spoke to all of them together. And they were all afraid, and fear and trembling came on them. ⁴And they earnestly pleaded with me to draw up a petition for them that they might find forgiveness, and for me to read their petition in the presence of the Lord of heaven. ⁵For from that time forward they could not speak with Him nor lift up their eyes to heaven for shame of their great errors and wrong for which they had been condemned.

⁶Then I wrote out their petition and prayer regarding their spirits and deeds individually and their requests that they should have forgiveness and length.

⁷And I went off and sat down at the waters in the land of Dan to the south west of Hermon, and I read their petition until I fell asleep. ⁸And a dream came to me, and visions fell down upon me, and I saw visions of punishment. And a voice came commanding me to tell this to the sons of heaven and reprimand them.

⁹And when I awoke, I went to them. They were all sitting together in Abelsjail, which is between Lebanon and Seneser, weeping with their faces covered. ¹⁰And I told them in detail all the visions that I had seen in sleep, and I began to speak the words about doing right and to reprimand the heavenly Watchers.

Chapter 14

The book of the words about doing right, and of the reprimand of the eternal Watchers in accordance with the command of the Holy Great One in that vision.

²"I saw in my sleep what I will now say, with a tongue of flesh and with the breath of my mouth, that which the Great One gave to Mankind to converse with and to understand with the heart. ³As He created and gave to Mankind the power of understanding the word of wisdom, so has He created me also and given me the authority to reprimand the Watchers, the children of heaven.

⁴"I wrote out your petition, and in my vision it was revealed to me that your petition will not be granted to you throughout all the days of eternity, and that final judg-

ment has been passed upon you. Your petition will not be granted to you. ⁵From this time on you will not ascend into heaven through out all eternity, and in bonds of the earth [you will remain]. The decree has gone forth to bind you for all the days of the world. ⁶Also before that, you will see the destruction of your beloved sons, and you will have no pleasure in them. They will fall before you by the sword. ⁷And your petition on their behalf will not be granted, and nothing you can do will change this, even though you weep and pray and speak all the words contained in the books I wrote."

⁸"And this is the vision shown to me: Look, in the vision, clouds invited me and a mist summoned me, and the course of the stars and the lightning sped and hurried me. The winds in the vision caused me to fly and lifted me upward and carried me into heaven.

⁹"I went in until I came near a wall built of crystals and surrounded by tongues of fire. And it began to frighten me. ¹⁰I went into the tongues of fire and near to a large house built of crystals. The walls of the house were like a mosaic floor of crystals, and its groundwork was of crystal. ¹¹Its ceiling was like the path of the stars and the lightning, and between them were fiery cherubim, and their sky was clear as water. ¹²A flaming fire surrounded the walls, and its doors blazed with fire. ¹³I entered into that house, and it was hot as fire and cold as ice. There were no delights of life in there. Fear covered me, and trembling got hold on me.

¹⁴"And as I quaked and trembled, I fell on my face. And I saw a vision, ¹⁵and there was a second house, greater than the former, and the entire door stood open before me, and it was built of flames of fire. ¹⁶And in every respect it so excelled in splendor, magnificence, and value that I cannot describe to you its splendor and its magnitude. ¹⁷Its floor was of fire, and above it were lightning

and the path of the stars. Its ceiling also was flaming fire.

[18]"And I looked in there and saw a high throne. Its appearance was as crystal, and its wheels were as the shining sun. There was the vision of cherubim. [19]From underneath the throne came streams of flaming fire so that I could not look at it. [20]And the Great Glory sat on the throne, and His raiment shone more brightly than the sun and was whiter than any snow. [21]None of the Messengers could enter and look on His face by reason of the magnificence and glory and no flesh could look on Him. [22]The flaming fire was round about Him, and a great fire stood before Him, and no one around could come near to Him. Ten thousand times ten thousand were before Him, yet He needed no counselor. [23]And the most holy ones who were near Him did not leave at night nor depart from Him.

[24]"And until then I had been prostrate on my face, trembling, and the Lord called me with His own mouth, and said to me: 'Come here, Enoch, and hear my word.'

[25]"And one of the set-apart ones came to me and woke me, and He made me rise up and approach the door, and I bowed my face downwards.

CHAPTER 15

"And the Lord answered and said to me, and I heard His voice:

" 'Do not be afraid, Enoch, you man of right doing and writer of what is right. Approach Me and hear my voice. [2]Go, say to the Watchers of heaven, who have sent you to intercede for them:

' "You should intercede for Mankind, and not Mankind for you. [3]Why have you left the high, set apart, and eternal heaven, and had intercourse with women, and defiled yourselves with the daughters of Mankind, and taken to yourselves wives, and done like the children of earth, and conceived giants as your sons?

⁴" "And though you were set-apart, spiritual, and living the eternal life, you defiled yourselves with the blood of women, and conceived children with the blood of flesh, and, like the children of men, lusted after flesh and blood like those who die and perish, ⁵which is why I gave them wives that they might impregnate them and produce children by them, so that nothing might be lacking to them on earth.

⁶" "But you were formerly spiritual, living the eternal life, and immortal for all generations of the world, ⁷which is why I have not appointed wives for you, because for the spiritual ones of heaven, heaven is their home."

⁸" 'And now, the giants, who are produced from the spirits and flesh, will be called evil spirits on the earth, and the earth will be their home. ⁹Evil spirits proceeded from their bodies because they are born from Mankind and from the set-apart Watchers. From this came their beginning and primary origin. They will be evil spirits on earth, and "evil spirits" they will be called.

¹⁰" 'As for the spirits of heaven, in heaven shall be their home. But for the spirits of the earth, which were born upon the earth, on the earth will be their dwelling.

¹¹" 'And the spirits of the giants [will continue to] afflict, oppress, destroy, attack, do battle, and work destruction on the earth, and cause trouble. But they take no food, even though they hunger, thirst, and cause offences. ¹²" 'And these spirits will rise up against the children of men and against the women, because they proceeded from them.

CHAPTER 16

" 'From the days of the slaughter, destruction, and death of the giants, from whose flesh the [evil] spirits have gone forth and these will corrupt [deceive] without incurring judgment - thus they will corrupt [deceive] until the day of their ultimate end, the great judgment in which the age will come to an end; until everything is concluded upon the Watchers and the godless.'

²" 'And now as to the Watchers who sent you to intercede for them, who before had been in heaven, say to them," ³'You have been in heaven, but all the mysteries had not yet been revealed to you, and you knew worthless ones. It was these, in the hardness of your hearts, you made known to the women, and through these mysteries women and men work much evil on earth.'

⁴" 'Say to them,' 'Therefore, you have no peace.' "

CHAPTER 17

And they took and brought me to a place in which those who were there were like flaming fire, and, when they wished, they appeared as men. ²They brought me to the place of darkness, and to a mountain the point of whose summit reached to heaven. ³And I saw the places of the luminaries and the treasuries of the stars and of the thunder and in the uttermost depths. Here was a fiery bow, arrows and their quiver, a fiery sword, and all the lightning.

⁴And they took me to the living waters, and to the fire of the west, which it receives from every setting of the sun. ⁵And I came to a river of fire in which the fire flows like water and discharges itself into the great sea towards the west. ⁶I saw the great rivers and came to the great river and to the great darkness, and went to the place where no flesh walks. ⁷I saw the mountains of the darkness of winter and the place from which all the waters of the deep flow. ⁸I saw the mouths of all the rivers of the earth and the mouth of the deep.

CHAPTER 18

I saw the treasuries of all the winds. I saw how He had furnished with them the whole creation and the firm foundations of the earth. ²And I saw the cornerstone of the earth. I saw the four winds that bear the earth and the firmament of the heaven. ³And I saw how the winds stretch out the vaults of heaven, and have their station between heaven and earth. These are the pillars of the heaven. ⁴I saw the winds of heaven, which turn and bring the circle of the sun and all the stars to their setting. ⁵I saw the winds on the earth carrying the clouds. I saw the paths of the Messengers. I saw at the end of the earth the firmament of the heaven above.

⁶And I proceeded and saw a place that burns day and night, where there are seven mountains of magnificent stones, three towards the east, and three towards the south. ⁷And those towards the east were of colored stone, and one of pearl, and one of jacinth, and those towards the south of red stone. ⁸But the middle one that reached to heaven like the throne of God, was of alabaster, and the summit of the throne was of sapphire. ⁹And I saw a flaming fire.

And beyond these mountains ¹⁰is a region, the end of the great earth, and there the heavens were completed. ¹¹And I saw a deep abyss, with columns of heavenly fire, and among them I saw columns of fire fall, which were beyond measure both to the height and to the depth. ¹²And beyond that abyss I saw a place that had no sky of the heaven above, and no firm foundation of earth beneath it. There was no water on it, and no birds. It was a waste and horrible place. ¹³In that place I saw seven stars like great burning mountains, and to me, when I inquired regarding them, ¹⁴the Messenger said,

"This place is the end of heaven and earth. This has
become a prison for the stars and the host of heaven.
¹⁵And the stars which roll over the fire are they which
have transgressed the commandment of the Lord in the
beginning of their rising, because they did not come forth
at their appointed times. ¹⁶And He was angry with them,
and bound them until the time when their guilt would be
complete: for ten thousand years."

CHAPTER 19
And Uriel said to me:

"Here shall stand the Messengers who had intercourse
with women, and their [demon] spirits assuming many
different forms are defiling Mankind and will lead them

astray into sacrificing to demons as gods, here will they stand, until the day of the great judgment in which they will be judged until they are brought to their ultimate end. ²And the women, also [born] of the Messengers who went astray, will become sirens."

³And I, Enoch, alone saw the vision, the ends of all things, and no man will see as I have seen.

CHAPTER 20

And these are the names of the set-apart Messengers who watch:

²• Uriel, one of the set-apart Messengers, who is over the world and over Tartarus.

³• Raphael, one of the set-apart Messengers, who is over the spirits of Mankind.

⁴• Raguel, one of the set-apart Messengers who takes vengeance on the world of the luminaries.

⁵• Michael, one of the set-apart Messengers. Know that he is set over the best part of Mankind and over chaos.

⁶• Saraqael, one of the set-apart Messengers, who is set over the spirits, who err in the spirit.

⁷• Gabriel, one of the set-apart Messengers, who is over Paradise, the serpents, and the Cherubim.

⁸• Remiel, one of the set-apart Messengers, whom God set over those who rise.

CHAPTER 21

I proceeded to where things were chaotic. ²And I saw there something horrible. I saw neither a sky above nor a firmly founded earth, but a chaotic and horrible place. ³And there I saw seven stars of the heaven bound together in it, like great mountains and burning with fire. ⁴Then I said: "For what sin are they bound, and on what account have they been cast in here?"

⁵Then Uriel, one of the set-apart Messengers, who was with me and was chief over them, said:

"Enoch, why do you ask, and why are you eager for the

truth? ⁶These are of the number of the stars of heaven that transgressed the commandment of the Lord, and they are bound here until ten thousand years, the time entailed by their serious errors, comes to its ultimate end."

⁷From there I went to another place that was still more horrible than the former. I saw a horrible thing there: a great fire that burned and blazed. And the place was cleft as far as the abyss, being full of great descending columns of fire, and neither its extent nor magnitude could I see, nor could I imagine. ⁸Then I said: "How fearful is the place and how terrible to look upon!"

⁹Then Uriel, one of the holy Messengers, who was with me, answered and said to me: "Enoch, why do you have such fear and are so afraid?"

And I answered, "Because of this fearful place, and because of the spectacle of the pain."

¹⁰And he said to me, "This place is the prison of the Messengers, and here they will be imprisoned forever."

CHAPTER 22

From there I went to another place, and he showed me in the west another great and high mountain of hard rock. ²And there was in it four hollow places, deep and wide and very smooth. How smooth are the hollow places and deep and dark to look at.

³Then Raphael, one of the holy Messengers, who was with me, answered and said to me:

> "These hollow places have been created for this very purpose, that the spirits of the souls of the dead should assemble therein, yea that all the [spirits of the] souls of the children of men should assemble here. ⁴And these places have been made to receive them until the day of their judgment and their appointed period, until the great judgment comes upon them."

⁵I saw the spirit of a dead man, making suit, and his voice went forth to heaven and made suit. ⁶And I asked Raphael the Messenger who was with me, "This spirit that makes suit, whose is it? Whose voice cries out and makes suit to heaven?"

⁷And he answered me,

> "This is the spirit that went out from Abel, whom Cain,
> his brother, murdered, and he makes his suit against him
> until his seed is destroyed from the face of the earth and
> annihilated from among the seed of men."

⁸Then I asked regarding it, and regarding all the hollow places: 'Why is one separated from the other?'

⁹And he answered,

> "These three have been made that the spirits of the
> dead might be separated. And such a division has been
> made for the spirits of the right-doers in which there is
> the bright spring of water. ¹⁰And such has been made for
> wrong-doers when they die and are buried in the earth
> and judgment has not been executed on them in their
> lifetime.

> ¹¹"Here their spirits shall be set apart in this great pain
> until the great day of judgment and punishment and tor-
> ment of those who curse for ever, and retribution for their
> spirits. There He shall bind them forever. ¹²Such a division
> has been made for the spirits of those who make their
> suit, who make disclosures concerning their destruction,
> when they were slain in the days of the wrong doers.

> ¹³"Such has been made for the spirits of men who were
> not right-doers but doers of what is wrong who were com-
> plete in transgression, and of the transgressors they will
> be companions. But their spirits will not be slain in the
> Day of Judgment nor shall they be raised from that place."

¹⁴Then I blessed the Lord of glory and said: "Blessed be my Lord, the Lord of right doing, who rules forever."

CHAPTER 23

From there I went to another place to the west of the ends of the earth. ²And I saw a burning fire that ran without resting, and did not stop from its course day or night but ran regularly. ³And I asked saying: "What is this which does not rest?"

⁴Then Raguel, one of the holy Messengers, who was with me, answered and said to me: "This course of fire, which you see, is the fire in the west that persecutes all the luminaries of heaven."

CHAPTER 24

From there I went to another place of the earth, and he showed me a mountain range of fire that burned day and night. ²And I went beyond it and saw seven magnificent mountains all different from each other, and the stones of these were magnificent and beautiful, magnificent as a whole, of glorious appearance and fair exterior: three towards the east, one founded on the other, and three towards the south, one upon the other, and deep rough ravines, no one of which joined with any other. ³And the seventh mountain was in the midst of these, and it excelled them in height, resembling the seat of a throne.

Fragrant trees encircled the throne. ⁴Among them was a tree such as I had never yet smelled, neither was any among them nor were others like it. It had a fragrance beyond all fragrances, and its leaves and blooms and wood never withered. Its fruit is beautiful, and its fruit resembles the dates of a palm.

⁵Then I said: "How beautiful is this tree, and fragrant, and its leaves are fair, and its blooms very delightful in appearance."

⁶Then Michael, one of the set-apart and honored Messengers who were with me and was their leader, answered,

CHAPTER 25

And said to me: "Enoch, why do you ask me regarding the fragrance of the tree, and why do you wish to learn the truth?"

²Then I answered him, "I wish to know about everything, but especially about this tree."

³And he answered,

> "This high mountain, which you have seen, whose
> summit is like the throne of God, is His throne, where the
> Set-apart Great One, the Lord of Glory, the Eternal King,
> will sit, when He shall come down to visit the earth with
> goodness.

⁴"As for this fragrant tree no mortal is permitted to touch it until the great judgment, when He shall take vengeance on all and bring everything to its ultimate conclusion forever. It shall then be given to the right-doers and to the set-apart. ⁵Its fruit shall be for food to the chosen. It will be transplanted to the set-apart place, to the temple of the Lord, the Eternal King. ⁶Then they will rejoice with joy and be glad, and enter into the set-apart place. Its fragrance will be in their bones. And they will live a long life on earth, like your fathers lived. In their days shall no sorrow, plague, torment, or calamity touch them."

⁷Then I blessed the God of Glory, the Eternal King, who prepared such things for the right-doers, created them, and promised to give these to them.

CHAPTER 26

I went from there to the middle of the earth, and I saw a blessed place in which there were trees with branches living and blooming from a dismembered tree. ²And there I saw a holy mountain, and underneath the mountain to the east there was a stream and it flowed towards the south.

³I saw towards the east another mountain higher than this, and between them a deep and narrow ravine, and in it also a stream ran underneath the mountain.

⁴To the west of this there was another mountain, lower than the former and of small elevation, and a ravine deep and dry between them, and another deep and dry ravine was at the extremities of the three mountains. ⁵And all the ravines were deep and narrow, formed of hard rock, and trees were not planted upon them. ⁶And I marveled at the rocks, and I marveled at the ravine, yes, I marveled very much.

CHAPTER 27

Then I said: 'What is purpose of this blessed land, which is entirely filled with trees, and this accursed valley between?'

²Then Uriel, one of the set-apart Messengers, who was with me, answered and said,

"This accursed valley is for those who are accursed forever. Here all the accursed will be gathered together, who utter unseemly words with their lips against the Lord, and of His glory, speak hard things. Here they will be gathered together, and here will be their place of judgment.

³"In the last days there will be upon them the spectacle of right judgment in the presence of the right-doers forever. Here will the merciful bless the Lord of glory, the Eternal King. ⁴In the days of judgment over the former, they will bless Him for the mercy in accordance with which He has assigned them their lot."

⁵Then I blessed the Lord of Glory and set forth His glory and praised Him gloriously.

CHAPTER 28

From there I went towards the east, into the midst of the mountain range of the desert, and I saw a wilderness and it was alone and full of trees and plants. ²And water gushed out from above. ³Rushing like a copious watercourse that flowed towards the northwest, it caused clouds and dew to ascend on every side.

CHAPTER 29

From there I went to another place in the desert, and approached to the east of this mountain range. ²There I saw aromatic trees exhaling the fragrance of frankincense and myrrh, and the trees also were similar to the almond tree.

CHAPTER 30

And beyond these, I went afar to the east, and I saw another place, a valley full of water. ²In there was a tree, the color of fragrant trees such as the mastic. ³And on the sides of those valleys I saw fragrant cinnamon. And beyond these I proceeded to the east.

CHAPTER 31

And I saw other mountains, and among them were groves of trees, and nectar flowed from them, which is named sarara and galbanum. ²Beyond these mountains I saw another mountain to the east of the ends of the earth, and on these were aloe-trees, and all the trees were full of oozing liquid, being like almond-trees. ³When one burnt it, it smelt sweeter than any fragrant odor.

CHAPTER 32

After these fragrant odors, as I looked towards the north over the mountains I saw seven mountains full of choice nard and fragrant trees and cinnamon and pepper. ²From there I went over the summits of all these mountains, far towards the east of the earth, and passed above the Erythraean sea and went far from it, and passed over the Messenger Zotiel.

³I came to the Garden of Righteousness, and saw beyond those trees many large trees of goodly fragrance, very beautiful and glorious, and he Tree of Wisdom [of good and evil] was there, from which those who eat gain great wisdom. ⁴That tree is in height like the fir, and its leaves are like those of the Carob tree, and its fruit is like the clusters of the vine, very beautiful, and the fragrance of the tree penetrates afar. ⁵Then I said: 'How beautiful is the tree, and how attractive is its look!'

⁶Then Raphael, the set-apart Messenger who was with me, answered me and said,

'This is the Tree of Wisdom [of good and evil], of which
your father, old in years, and your aged mother, who were
before you, have eaten, and they learned wisdom, and
their eyes were opened, and they knew that they were naked, and they were driven out of the garden.'

CHAPTER 33

From there I went to the ends of the earth and saw there great beasts different from each other; and I saw birds also differing in appearance and beauty and voice, each one different from the others. ²To the east of those beasts I saw the ends of the earth whereon the heaven rests, and the doors of the heaven open.

³And I saw how the stars of heaven come forth, and I counted the doors

out of which they proceed, and wrote down all their outlets, of each individual star by itself, according to their number and their names, their courses and their positions, their times and their months, as Uriel, the set-apart Messenger who was with me, showed me.

⁴He showed all things to me and wrote them down for me. He also wrote for me their names, laws, and companies.

CHAPTER 34

From there I went towards the north to the ends of the earth, and there I saw a great and glorious device at the ends of the whole earth. ²Here I saw three doors of heaven open in the heaven and through each of them comes north winds. When they blow [on earth] there is cold, hail, frost, snow, dew, and rain. ³And out of one door they blow for good. But when they blow through the other two doors, they create violence and affliction on the earth, and they blow with violence.

CHAPTER 35

From there I went towards the west to the ends of the earth, and saw there three doors of the heaven open such as I had seen in the east, the same number of portals, and the same number of outlets.

CHAPTER 36

From there I went to the south to the ends of the earth, and saw three open portals of the heaven: and from these came dew, rain, and wind. ²From there I went to the east to the ends of the heaven, and saw here the three eastern doors of heaven open and small portals above them. ³Through each of these small portals pass the stars of heaven and run their course to the west on the path that is shown to them.

⁴As often as I saw I blessed always the Lord of Glory, and I continued to bless the Lord of Glory who has wrought great and glorious wonders, to show the greatness of His work to the Messenger, to spirits, and to Mankind, that they might praise His work and all His creation that they might see the work of His might and praise the great work of His hands and bless Him for ever.

The Book of Parables

W here the Book of the Watchers focused on current events in Enoch's time and their effect on our future, "The Book of the Parables" looks directly at our future. If I were to give this a subtitle, I think it would be "The Gospel of Enoch."

This contains wisdom directed "to those that dwell on the earth." There are three "parables" in this book, but other documents are also found including a fragment of Noah, who, you could imagine, found plenty of time available to recount these events and write them for us.

The First Parable sets the time of events yet in our future, when the "congregation of the righteous [*those who do what is right*] will *appear.*" Following John's vision of Revelation 2 and 3, the "congregation" contains all – from the time of Adam to the end of the first seven ages – who "overcame" the world. This raises the question – "after the righteous *appear,*" what happens to the rest. This is the theme for this book.

In this and all the books of Enoch, "elect" means "chosen" and, in some places, "set-apart." It has nothing to do with politics or voting. The "elect" are those that have been "chosen" by the "Lord of Spirits." The "elect" come from among Mankind by "promises and covenants" between our fathers and the One who is called "the Elect [Chosen] One" who is the One who made and upholds these covenants.

The vision of the future world led Enoch to exclaim,

"There I wished to dwell, and my spirit longed for *that* dwelling place."

Enoch also saw Michael, Raphael, Gabriel, and Phanuel, all powerful Messengers. And other visions gave Enoch insight into the order and working of the creation and of Heaven, where prayers and intercession are made "for those who dwell on the earth."

The Second Parable is another vision of future events and forms the foundation of the prophecies given to the prophets and to the true apostles. Here you learn how the earth and its people have fallen under a curse that will come to its appointed end. Enoch saw the changes that will happen to restore the heaven and make it "an eternal blessing and light," and to the earth and "make it a blessing."

Enoch writes about a clear distinction between those who do right and the elect, and "those who do wrong and those who *plan* to do wrong." This is often misunderstood because the translator used the word "sinners" and "evil-doers" – words that are defined by religious dogma and not by Scripture.

The Third Parable concerns "the righteous [doers of right] and the elect [chosen]" and how they will fare in the "world to come." The dwelling place of the those who do what is right and the elect is a "clean" place. "Those who do wrong and those who plan to do wrong [evil-doers]" could not live there – even if they tried!

To say that "those who do wrong and those who plan to do wrong" will not exist is true. Because, as Enoch saw, those who live this way, at sometime during their *Lifetime,* will change and become those who do right!

This becomes the message of Enoch, and of the rest of the Scriptures.

The fulfillment of this promise does not lie in the hands of the Mankind, but the "Son of Man" will remove the "kings and mighty from their seats and the strong from their thrones." He is the deliverer, who will come and clean the earth and make it, along with the heavens, a place where the right-doers can live: "In those days a change will take place ... "

The good news is stated in Chapter 50. Because "the right-doers will be victorious in the Name of the Lord of Spirits," He will cause the others (evil-doers and those who do wrong) to *witness* this "*that they may repent and leave the works of their hands*" – a far cry from current evangelical thought, isn't it?

The message of the Good News or Gospel is never more clear than in the revelations given to Enoch, but it does conflict with what one might hear on Sunday morning or in a *revival* meeting, doesn't it? Can you begin to see why the religions did not want Enoch to influence their theology?

A discourse in Chapter 61 shows the power of the Elect One and how the "right-doers" will be fixed like a mast to a boat so that they can sail through the time of judgment and tribulation. This is an interesting and comforting vision of the protection they will be given, isn't it?

Another theme that carries through the Book of Parables is the Hidden Son of Man. Even during our time His identity is still hidden and few know who He is. Although many think they know, the rest of the world just isn't buying it. But the day is coming, as the writing of Enoch shows, that the "right-doers" and the chosen [elect] "will be saved on that day."

> "The right-doers and the elect will have risen from the earth, and ceased to be downcast in spirit. They will have been clothed with garments of glory [esteem]. These will be garments of Life from the Lord of Spirits."

THE WANDERING DESTROYER

Chapters 65 through 69 are not Enoch's writing, but belong to his great grandson, Noah. This fascinating section appears to have puzzled the translators and only until recently can we begin to get a glimpse into Noah's concern about the earth. Prior to the flood the earth began to shake and roll. Noah became concerned that the land was actually sinking. The translators, however were unaware of the very high probability that our solar system is part of a binary star system. In other words, the sun has a companion sun that "wanders" around our solar system in a very large elliptical orbit. NASA determined that about 80% of all solar systems in the universe are binary.

Some called the other half of our system "planet x" or "nibiru" from other ancient writings. However, it appears that this "wandering" system is most likely a brown dwarf star with its own planets. It has been called the "Destroyer." In the book of Revelation, John wrote that its name in Hebrew is Abadden ("wandering destroyer") and in Greek, Apollyn ("destroyer"). It is also referred to as a great red dragon, and a king over the first 5 trumpets. Its appearence in the sky is that of a second sun, that emerges out of the "abyss" or the depths of the universe, and brings destruction to the earth.

Prior to its arrival the earth will begin to feel the power of its gravitation and begin to shake and roll. This is similar to what Noah experienced that drove him to seek the answers from his great-grandfather Enoch. Noah also made reference to an anticipated "impact," which was missed by Charles and picked up by Charlesworth. Although a direct impact with the earth would destroy the earth. A close "fly-by" is sufficient to cause major problems that will completely change life as we know it. This is what the prophecies of the "first end" foretold and the "second end" foretell. In my early writings I wondered what power caused the waters above to come down on the earth. I thought that a fly-by of possibly an asteroid may have cause that, but I was never satisfed with that. But now following the discovery of a brown dwarf star in our universe, the answer becomes very clear.

Enoch was told that the calendar revealed to him would remain in force until the new heavens and new earth. It is anticipated that this brown dwarf star will begin to be visible in early 2009, and start to reak havoc on the earth as John saw in his visions of the seven trumpets. Some scientists believe that about 4,000 years from now, when this sister star appears again, it will impact with our sun and destroy our solar system, as Peter prophesied (II Peter 3.) But this will have no impact on those who are living the eternal life, which will begin to be realized in the Eighth Week (age) of Enoch's vision of the Weeks.

THE GOSPEL OF ENOCH

His words repeat the *gospel* of Enoch saying, "From that time [the next age] on, *there will be nothing corruptible*, for that Son of Man has appeared and has seated Himself on the throne of His glory."

This Book concludes with a description of Enoch's ascension "into the heavens," and with a summary of the good news given to Enoch by a Messenger,

> "He proclaims to you peace in the name *of the world
> to come ... All will walk in His ways* because doing what is
> right never leaves Him."

As this Book of Parables demonstrates, Enoch's visions, writings, messages, and revelations are the Key to all Scriptures.

The Book of Parables

Chapter 37

The second vision that he saw, the vision of wisdom that Enoch the son of Jared, the son of Mahalalel, the son of Cainan, the son of Enos, the son of Seth, the son of Adam, saw. ²This is the beginning of the words of wisdom that I lifted up my voice to speak and say to those that live on the earth.

> Hear, you men of old time, and see, you that come after, the words of the Set-apart One that I will speak before the Lord of Spirits. ³It were better to declare them only to the men of old time, but even from those that come after *we will not withhold the beginning of wisdom.* ⁴Until the present day the Lord of Spirits has never given such wisdom as I have received according to my insight, according to the good pleasure of the Lord of Spirits who has given the lot of eternal life to me.

⁵Now three Parables were revealed to me, and I lifted up my voice and told them in detail *to those that live on the earth.*

Chapter 38

The First Parable: When the congregation of the righteous [those who do what is right] *will appear,* and sinners [those who do wrong] will be judged for their sins [wrong doings] and driven from the face of the earth, ²and when the One Who Does What is Right will appear before the eyes of those who do what is right, whose chosen works hang upon the Lord of Spirits, light will appear to those who do what is right and to the elect [chosen] who live on the earth, where then will be the living place of those who do wrong and the place of resting for those who have denied the Lord of Spirits? It had been good for them if they had not been born.

³When the secrets of those who do right will be revealed and the wrongdoers judged, and the godless driven from the presence of the right-doers and the elect, ⁴from that time those that possess the earth will no longer be powerful and exalted, and they will not be able to look upon the face of the set-apart.

For the Lord of Spirits has caused His light to appear on the face of the set-apart, the right-doers, and the chosen. ⁵Then the kings and the "powerful" will die and be given into the hands of the right-doers and set-apart, ⁶and from that time on none [of the kings and powerful] will seek for themselves mercy from the Lord of Spirits for their life is at an end.

CHAPTER 39

It came to pass in those days that elect [chosen] and set-apart children [the Watchers] descended from the high heaven, and their seed became one with the children of men.

²Also in those days Enoch received books of passion and anger, and books of overwhelming fear and expelling. "Mercy will not be accorded to them [the Watchers]," says the Lord of Spirits.

³In those days a whirlwind carried me off the earth and set me down at the end of the heavens. ⁴There I saw another vision, the dwelling places of the set-apart, and the resting places of the right-doers. ⁵My eyes saw their dwellings with His right-doing Messengers, and their resting-places with the set-apart. And they petitioned, interceded, and prayed for the children of men, and right doing flowed before them as water, and mercy like dew upon the earth. Thus it is among them forever and ever.

⁶In that place I saw the Elect One of right doing and of faith. ⁷And I saw his dwelling place under the wings of the Lord of Spirits. Doing right will prevail in his days; and the right-doers and chosen will be without number before Him forever and ever.

All the right-doers and chosen before Him will be strong as fiery lights, and their mouth will be full of blessing, and their lips praise highly the name of the Lord of Spirits. Right doing before Him will never fail, and uprightness will never fail before Him.

⁸*There I wished to dwell, and my spirit longed for that dwelling-place.* And there, up to this time, has been my portion, for so has it been established concerning me before the Lord of Spirits.

⁹In those days I praised and honored the name of the Lord of Spirits with blessings and praises, because He has destined me for blessing and high esteem according to the good pleasure of the Lord of Spirits. ¹⁰For a long time my eyes regarded that place, and I blessed Him and praised

Him, saying,

> "Blessed is He. May He be blessed from the beginning
> and for evermore. [11]Before Him there is no end. He knows
> before the world was created what is forever and what
> will be from generation to generation. [12]Those who do not
> sleep bless you. They stand before Your glory and bless,
> praise, and extol, saying, 'Set-apart, set-apart, set-apart,
> is the Lord of Spirits. He fills the earth with spirits.' "

[13]Here I saw all those who do not sleep. They stand before Him and bless and say,

> "Blessed be You. Blessed be the name of the Lord for-
> ever and ever."

[14]And my face was changed, for I could no longer look.

CHAPTER 40

After that I saw thousands of thousands and ten thousand times ten thousand. I saw a multitude beyond number and reckoning that stood before the Lord of Spirits. [2]On the four sides of the Lord of Spirits I saw four presences, different from those that do not sleep, and I learned their names because the Messenger that went with me made known to me their names, and showed me all the hidden things. [3]And I heard the voices of those four presences as they uttered praises before the Lord of glory [worthy of great respect and honor].

- [4]• The first voice blesses the Lord of Spirits forever and ever.
- [5]• The second voice I heard blessing the Elect One and the
  elect ones who hang upon the Lord of Spirits.
- [6]• The third voice I heard pray and intercede for those who
  dwell on the earth and supplicate in the name of the Lord
  of Spirits.
- [7]• And I heard the fourth voice fending off the adversaries
  and forbidding them to come before the Lord of Spirits to
  accuse those who dwell on the earth.

[8]After that I asked the Messenger of peace who went with me, who showed me everything that is hidden, "Who are these four Presences, which I have seen and whose words I have heard and written down?"

⁹ And he said to me,

>This first is Michael, the merciful and long-suffering.
>
>The second, who is set over all the diseases and all the wounds of the children of men, is Raphael.
>
>The third, who is set over all the powers, is Gabriel.
>
>And the fourth, who is set over the repentant unto hope of those who inherit eternal life, is named Phanuel.

¹⁰These are the four Messengers of the Lord of Spirits and the four voices I heard in those days.

CHAPTER 41

After that I saw all the secrets of the heavens, and how the kingdom is divided, and how the actions of men are weighed in the balance.

²There I saw the mansions of the elect and the mansions of the set-apart, and I saw there all the wrong-doers being driven from there who deny the name of the Lord of Spirits and being dragged off, and they could not stay there because of the punishment that proceeds from the Lord of Spirits.

³There my eyes saw the secrets of the lightning and of the thunder, and the secrets of the winds, how they are divided to blow over the earth, and the secrets of the clouds and dew, and there I saw from where they proceed in that place and from where they saturate the dusty earth.

⁴And there I saw closed chambers out of which the winds are divided, the chamber of the hail and winds, the chamber of the mist, and of the clouds, and the cloud hovers over the earth from the beginning of the world.

⁵And I saw the chambers of the sun and moon, from where they proceed and how they come again, and their glorious return, and how one is superior to the other, and their stately orbit, and how they do not leave their orbit, and they add nothing to their orbit and they take nothing from it, and they keep faith with each other, in accordance with the oath by which they are bound together.

⁶And first the sun goes and traverses his path according to the commandment of the Lord of Spirits, and mighty is His name forever and ever.

⁷After that I saw the hidden and the visible path of the moon, and she

accomplishes the course of her path in that place by day and by night - the one holding a position opposite to the other before the Lord of Spirits. And they give thanks and praise and rest not, for to them is their thanksgiving rest. ⁸For the sun changes often for a blessing or a curse, and the course of the path of the moon is light to the right-doers and darkness to the wrong-doers in the name of the Lord who made a separation between the light and the darkness and divided the spirits of men, and strengthened the spirits of the right-doers in the name of His Righteousness. ⁹For no Messenger hinders and no power is able to hinder, for He appoints a judge for all and He judges all of them before Him.

CHAPTER 42

Wisdom found no place where she might dwell. Then a dwelling place was assigned her in the heavens. ²Wisdom went out from there to make her dwelling among the children of men, and found no dwelling place. Wisdom returned to her place, and took her seat among the Messengers, ³and wrong doing went away from her chambers. Whom she did not seek she found, and lived with them, as rain in a desert and dew on a thirsty land.

CHAPTER 43

I saw other lightning and the stars of heaven, and I saw how He called them all by their names and they listened to Him. ²And I saw how they are weighed in a correct and precise balance according to their proportions of light. I saw the width of their spaces and the day of their appearing, and how their revolution produces lightning. And I saw their revolution according to the number of the Messengers, and how they keep faith with each other. ³And I asked the Messenger who went with me who showed me what was hidden, "What are these?"

⁴And he said to me:

"The Lord of Spirits has shown you their parable.
These are the names of the set-apart who dwell on the
earth and believe in the name of the Lord of Spirits forever and ever."

CHAPTER 44

Another phenomenon I saw in regard to the lightning: How some of the stars arise and become lightning and cannot part with their new form.

CHAPTER 45

This is the Second Parable: Concerning those who deny the name of the dwelling of the set-apart ones and the Lord of Spirits. ²Into the heaven they will not ascend, and on the earth they will not come. Such will be the lot of the wrong-doers who have denied the name of the Lord of Spirits, who are thus preserved for the day of suffering and tribulation.

³"On that day My Elect One will sit on the throne of honor and high esteem, and will try their works, and their places of rest will be innumerable. And their souls will grow strong within them when they see My Elect Ones and those who have called upon My glorious [worthy of great respect and honor] Name.

⁴"Then I will cause My Elect One to dwell among them. I will transform the heaven and make it an eternal blessing and light, ⁵and I will transform the earth and make it a blessing. And I will cause My elect ones to dwell upon it.

"But the doers of wrong and the those who plan and carry-out wrong doing will not set foot on it. ⁶For I have provided and satisfied with peace My right-doing ones and have caused them to dwell before Me. But for the wrong-doers there is judgment impending with Me, so that I will destroy them from the face of the earth."

CHAPTER 46

There I saw One who had a head of days. His head was white like wool, and with Him was another being whose countenance had the appearance of a man, and his face was full of graciousness, like one of the set-apart Messengers.

²I asked the Messenger who went with me and showed me all the hidden things, concerning that Son of Man, who He was, and where He was, and why He went with the Head of Days.

³He answered me,

"This is the Son of Man who has righteousness, with whom dwells righteousness, and who reveals all the treasures of that which is hidden because the Lord of Spirits has chosen him and whose lot has the pre-eminence before the Lord of Spirits in uprightness forever.

⁴"This Son of Man whom you have seen will lift up the kings and the mighty from their seats and the strong from their thrones, and will loosen the reins of the strong and break the teeth of the wrong-doers. ⁵He will put down the kings from their thrones and kingdoms, because they do not extol and praise Him, nor humbly acknowledge from whom and from where the kingdom was bestowed upon them.

⁶"He will put down the countenance of the strong and will fill them with shame. Darkness will be their dwelling and worms will be their bed. They will have no hope of rising from their beds because they do not extol the name of the Lord of Spirits. ⁷These are they who judge the stars of heaven, and raise their hands against the Most High, and tread upon the earth and dwell upon it.

"All their deeds create wrong results, and their power rests on their riches. Their faith is in the gods that they made with their hands, and at the same time they deny the name of the Lord of Spirits. ⁸They persecute the houses of His congregations and the faithful who hang upon the name of the Lord of Spirits."

CHAPTER 47

In those days will ascend the prayer of the right-doers, and the blood of the right-doers from the earth before the Lord of Spirits. ²In those days the set-apart ones who dwell above in the heavens will unite with one voice and supplicate, pray, praise, give thanks, and bless the name of the Lord of Spirits on behalf of the blood of the right-doers that was shed, and pray that the prayer of the right-doers may not be in vain before the Lord of

Spirits, and that judgment may be done to them that they may not have to suffer forever.

³In those days I saw the Head of Days when He seated himself upon the throne of His glory, and the books of the living were opened before Him. All His host that is in heaven above and His counselors stood before Him, ⁴and the hearts of the set-apart were filled with joy because the number of the right-doers had been offered, and the prayer of the right-doers had been heard, and the blood of the right-doers been required before the Lord of Spirits.

CHAPTER 48

In that place I saw the fountain of right doing that was inexhaustible. Many fountains of wisdom were around it. All the thirsty drank from them and were filled with wisdom. Their dwellings were with the right-doers and set-apart and elect.

²And at that hour the Son of Man was named in the presence of the Lord of Spirits and his name before the Head of Days. ³Yes, before the sun and the signs were created, before the stars of the heaven were made, His name was named before the Lord of Spirits.

⁴He will be a staff to [all] the right-doer whereon to support themselves and not fall. He will be the light of the nations and the hope of those who are troubled of heart. ⁵All who dwell on earth will fall down and worship before him, and will praise, bless, and celebrate with song the Lord of Spirits. ⁶For this reason has He [the Son of Man] been chosen and hidden before Him, before the creation of the world and for evermore.

⁷And the wisdom of the Lord of Spirits revealed him to the set-apart and right-doers for he has preserved the lot of the right-doers because they hated and despised this world of doing wrong and hated all its works and ways in the name of the Lord of Spirits. For *in his name [the Son of Man] they are saved* and according to his good pleasure has it been in regard to their life.

⁸In these days the kings of the earth will become downcast in face, and the strong, which possess the land, because of the works of their hands. For on the day of their anguish and affliction they will not be able to save themselves.

9"And I will give them over into the hands of My elect [chosen]. As straw in the fire so they will burn before the face of the set-apart. As lead in the water they will sink before the face of the right-doers, and no trace of them will be found any more. 10On the day of their affliction, there will be rest on the earth and before them [the right-doers], they will fall and not rise again. And there will be no one to take them with his hands and raise them for they denied the Lord of Spirits and His Anointed. "

Blessed be the name of the Lord of Spirits ...

CHAPTER 49
For wisdom is poured out like water, and glory does not fail before Him forever. 2For He is mighty in all the secrets of doing right, and doing wrong will disappear as a shadow and have no duration, because the Elect One stands before the Lord of Spirits and His glory is forever and ever. His might endures to all generations. 3In Him dwells the spirit of wisdom, the spirit that gives insight, the spirit of understanding and might, and the spirit of those who have fallen asleep in right-doing.

4And He will judge the secret things, and no one will be able to say a lying word before Him. For He is the Elect [Chosen] One before the Lord of Spirits according to His good pleasure.

CHAPTER 50
In those days a change will take place for the set-apart and elect, and the light of days will come upon them. Glory and honor will turn to the set-apart 2on the day of affliction on which evil will have been treasured up against the sinners.

The right-doers will be victorious in the name of the Lord of Spirits, and He will cause the others to witness this that they may repent and leave the works of their hands. 3They will have no honor through the name of the Lord of Spirits. *Yet through His name they will be saved*, and the Lord of Spirits will have compassion on them, for His compassion is great.

4He does right also in His judgment. In the presence of His glory wrong doing also will not maintain itself. At His judgment the unrepentant {unchanging and inflexible] will perish before Him.

⁵"From that time on I will have no mercy on them," says the Lord of Spirits.

CHAPTER 51
Also in those days the earth will give back that which has been entrusted to it. Sheol [the grave] will also give back what it has received. And hell [the grave] will give back what it owes. For in those days the Elect One will arise, ²and he shall choose the right-doers and set-apart from among them. For the day has drawn near that they should be saved.

> ³"The Elect One will in those days sit on My throne,
> and His mouth shall pour forth all the secrets of wisdom
> and counsel, for the Lord of Spirits has given them to Him
> and has glorified Him. ⁴In those days the mountains will
> leap like rams, and the hills also will skip like lambs satis-
> fied with milk. The faces of all the Messengers in heaven
> will be lighted up with joy. ⁵The earth will rejoice, and the
> right-doers will dwell on it, and the elect will walk on it."

CHAPTER 52
After those days in that place where I had seen all the visions of that which is hidden – for I had been carried off in a whirlwind and they carried me towards the west. ²There my eyes saw all the secret things of heaven that will be, a mountain of iron, a mountain of copper, a mountain of silver, a mountain of gold, a mountain of soft metal, and a mountain of lead. ³And I asked the Messenger who went with me, "What are these things that I have seen in secret?"

⁴And he said to me,

> "All these things that you have seen will serve the do-
> minion of His Anointed that he may be potent and mighty
> on the earth."

⁵And that Messenger of peace answered me,

> "Wait a little, and there will be revealed to you all
> the secret things that surround the Lord of Spirits. ⁶And

these mountains that your eyes have seen, the mountain of iron, the mountain of copper, the mountain of silver, the mountain of gold, the mountain of soft metal, and the mountain of lead, will be in the presence of the Elect One as wax before the fire and like the water that streams down from above upon those mountains. And they will all become powerless before his feet.

7"It will happen in those days that none will be saved, either by gold or by silver, and none will be able to escape. 8And there will be no iron for war. Nor will one clothe oneself with a breastplate. Bronze will be of no service, and tin will be of no service and will not be valued. Lead will not be desired. 9All these things will be denied and destroyed from the surface of the earth, when the Elect One will appear before the face of the Lord of Spirits."

CHAPTER 53

There my eyes saw a deep valley with open mouths, and all who dwell on the earth, sea, and islands will bring to him [the Adversary] gifts, presents, and tokens of homage, but that deep valley will not become full.

2Their hands commit lawless deeds, and the wrong-doers devour all whom they lawlessly oppress. Yet the wrong-doers will be destroyed before the face of the Lord of Spirits, and they will be banished from off the face of His earth. They will perish forever and ever.

3I saw all the Messengers of punishment living there and preparing all the instruments of Satan [the Advesary]. 4And I asked the Messenger of peace who went with me, "For whom are they preparing these instruments?"

5And he said to me,

"They prepare these for the kings and the mighty of this earth that they may be destroyed by these. 6After this the Right-doer and Elect One will cause the house of His congregation to appear, and from then on they will not be hindered in the name of the Lord of Spirits.

7"These mountains [nations] will not stand as the earth

before His right doing, but the hills will be as a fountain of water, and the right-doers will have rest from the oppression of sinners."

Chapter 54

I looked and turned to another part of the earth, and saw there a deep valley with burning fire. ²And they brought the kings and the mighty and began to cast them into this deep valley. ³There my eyes saw how they made these their instruments, iron chains of immeasurable weight. ⁴And I asked the Messenger of peace who went with me, "For whom are these chains being prepared?"

⁵And he said to me,

> "These are being prepared for the armies of Azazel, so that they may take them and cast them into the abyss of complete condemnation. They will cover their jaws with rough stones as the Lord of Spirits commanded.
>
> ⁶"Michael, Gabriel, Raphael, and Phanuel will take hold of them on that great day and cast them into the burning furnace that the Lord of Spirits may take vengeance on them for their unrighteousness in becoming subject to Satan [the Adverary] and leading astray those who dwell on the earth.
>
> ⁷"In those days punishment will come from the Lord of Spirits, and he will open all the chambers of waters that are above the heavens and the fountains that are beneath the earth. ⁸And all the waters will be joined with the waters.
>
> "That which is above the heavens is the masculine, and the water that is beneath the earth is the feminine. ⁹And they will destroy all who dwell on the earth and those who dwell under the ends of the heaven. ¹⁰And when they have recognized their unrighteousness that they have created on the earth then by these will they perish."

CHAPTER 55

After that the Head of Days repented and said, "In vain have I destroyed all who dwell on the earth."

²And He swore by His great name,

> "From now on, I will not do so to all who dwell on the earth, and I will set a sign in the heaven, and this will be a pledge of good faith between Me and them forever, so long as heaven is above the earth. And this is in accordance with My command. ³When I have desired to take hold of them by the hand of the Messengers on the day of tribulation and pain because of this, I will cause My chastisement and My wrath to abide upon them," says Elah, the Lord of Spirits.

> ⁴"You mighty kings who dwell on the earth, you will have to behold My Elect One, how he sits on the throne of glory and judges Azazel, all his associates, and all his hosts [armies] in the name of the Lord of Spirits."

CHAPTER 56

And I saw there the hosts of the Messengers of punishment going, and they held scourges and chains of iron and bronze. ²And I asked the Messenger of peace that went with me, "To whom are these going, who hold the scourges?"

³And he said to me,

> "To their elect and beloved ones that they may be cast into the chasm of the abyss of the valley. ⁴And then that valley will be filled with their elect and beloved. And the days of their lives will be at an end. From then on the days of their leading astray will not be counted.

> ⁵"And in those days the Messengers will return and hurl themselves to the east upon the Parthians [related to the Persians (Iran)] and Medes [also Iran].[a scribe entry]. They will stir up the kings, so that a spirit of unrest will come on them, and they will rouse them from their thrones that they may break forth as lions from their lairs,

and as hungry wolves among their flocks. [6]And they will go up and tread under foot the land of His elect [chosen] ones, and the land of His elect ones will be before them a threshing floor and a highway.

[7]But the city of my righteous will be a hindrance to their horses. And they will begin to fight among themselves. Their right hand will be strong against themselves, and a man will not know his brother, nor a son his father or his mother, until there be innumerable corpses through their slaughter, and their punishment will not be in vain.

[8]In those days Sheol [the grave] will open its jaws, and they will be swallowed up, and their destruction will be at an end. Sheol will devour the doers of wrong in the presence of the elect."

CHAPTER 57

It came to pass after this that I saw another host of wagons, and men riding on them and coming on the winds from the east and the west to the south. [2]And the noise of their wagons was heard, and when this turmoil took place, the set-apart ones from heaven remarked about it. The pillars of the earth were moved from their place, and the sound was heard from the one end of heaven to the other in one day. [3]And they will all fall down and worship the Lord of Spirits.

This completes the end of the Second Parable.

CHAPTER 58

I began to speak the Third Parable: Concerning the righteous and elect:

[2]"Blessed are you, you righteous and elect, for glorious will be your lot. [3]The righteous will be in the light of the sun, and the elect in the light of eternal life. The days of *their life will be unending*, and the days of the set-apart without number. [4]They will seek the light and find righteousness with the Lord of Spirits. There will be peace to

the righteous in the name of the Eternal Lord.

⁵"After this it will be said to the set-apart in heaven that they should seek out the secrets of righteousness, the heritage of faith, for it has become bright as the sun upon earth. The darkness is past, ⁶and there will be a light that never ends, and to a limit of days they will not come, for the darkness will first be destroyed and light established before the Lord of Spirits, and the light of uprightness [will be] established forever before the Lord of Spirits."

CHAPTER 59

In those days my eyes saw the secrets of the lightning, of the lights, and the judgments they execute. They lighten for a blessing or a curse as the Lord of Spirits wills. ²There I also saw the secrets of the thunder, and how when it resounds above in the heaven the sound is heard.

He caused me to see the judgments executed on the earth whether they be for well-being and blessing or for a curse according to the word of the Lord of Spirits. ³After that, all the secrets of the lights and lightning were shown to me, and they lighten for blessing and for satisfying.

CHAPTER 60

In the year five hundred, in the seventh month, on the fourteenth day of the month in the life of Enoch. In that Parable I saw how a mighty quaking made the heaven of heavens to quake, and the armies of the Most High, and the Messengers, a thousand thousands and ten thousand times ten thousand were disturbed with a great turmoil.

²The Head of Days sat on the throne of His glory, and the Messengers and the righteous stood around Him. ³And a great trembling seized me and fear took hold of me. My loins gave way and dissolved were my reins, and I fell upon my face.

⁴Michael sent another Messenger from among the set-apart ones, and he raised me up. When he had raised me up my spirit returned, for I had not been able to endure the look of this army, the commotion, and the quaking of the heaven. ⁵And Michael said to me,

"Why are you so unsettled with such a vision? Until

this day lasted the day of His mercy and He has been merciful and patient towards those who live on the earth. [6]And when the day, the power, the punishment, and the judgment come, which the Lord of Spirits prepared for those who do not worship the righteous law, for those who deny the righteous judgment, and for those who take His name in vain, that day is prepared. It is for the elect [chosen] a covenant, but for doers of wrong an inquisition.

"When the punishment of the Lord of Spirits will rest on them, it will rest in order that the punishment of the Lord of Spirits may not come in vain, and it will slay the children with their mothers and the children with their fathers. Afterwards the judgment will take place according to His mercy and His patience."

[7]And on that day two monsters were parted. A female monster named Leviathan was assigned to dwell in the abysses of the ocean over the fountains of the waters.

[8]The male named Behemoth occupied with his breast a waste wilderness named Duidain on the east of the garden where the elect and righteous dwell, where my grandfather was taken up. He was the seventh from Adam, the first man whom the Lord of Spirits created.

[9]I pleaded with the other Messenger that he should show me the might of those monsters, how they were parted on one day and cast, the one into the abysses of the sea, and the other unto the dry land of the wilderness.

[10]He said to me, "You son of man, do you seek to know what is hidden?"

[11]And the other Messenger, who went with me and showed me what was hidden, told me what is first and last in the heaven in the height, beneath the earth in the depth, at the ends of the heaven, and on the foundation of the heaven.

[12]And the chambers of the winds, how the winds are divided, how they are weighed, and how the portals [doors] of the winds are reckoned, each according to the power of the wind, the power of the lights of the moon, and according to the power that is fitting, the divisions of the stars accord-

ing to their names, and how all the divisions are divided.

[13]And the thunders according to the places where they fall, and all the divisions that are made among the lightning that it may lighten, and their host that they may at once obey. [14]For the thunder has places of rest that are assigned to it while it is waiting for its peal. The thunder and lightning are inseparable, and although not one and undivided, they both go together through the spirit and separate not. [15]For when the lightning lightens, the thunder utters its voice, and the spirit enforces a pause during the peal, and divides equally between them; for the treasury of their peals is like the sand, and each one of them as it peals is held in with a bridle, and turned back by the power of the spirit, and pushed forward according to the many quarters of the earth.

[16]The spirit of the sea is masculine and strong, and according to the might of his strength he draws it back with a rein, and in like manner it is driven forward and disperses amid all the mountains of the earth.

[17]The spirit of the hoarfrost is his own Messenger, and the spirit of the hail is a good Messenger. [18]The spirit of the snow has forsaken his chambers on account of his strength. There is a special spirit therein, and that which ascends from it is like smoke, and its name is frost. [19]And the spirit of the mist is not united with them in their chambers, but it has a special chamber; for its course is glorious both in light and in darkness, and in winter and in summer, and in its chamber is a Messenger. [20]And the spirit of the dew has its dwelling at the ends of the heaven, and is connected with the chambers of the rain, and its course is in winter and summer: and its clouds and the clouds of the mist are connected, and the one gives to the other.

[21]When the spirit of the rain goes out from its chamber, the Messengers come and open the chamber and lead it out, and when it is diffused over the whole earth it unites with the water on the earth. And whenever it unites with the water on the earth, [22]for the waters are for those who live on the earth; for they are nourishment for the earth from the Most High who is in heaven. Therefore there is a measure for the rain, and the Messengers take it in charge. [23]And these things I saw towards the Garden of the Right-Doers. [24]And the Messenger of peace who was with me said to me, "These two monsters, prepared conformably to the greatness of Elah,

shall feed."

CHAPTER 61

I saw in those days how long cords were given to those Messengers, and they took to themselves wings and flew and went towards the north. ²I asked the Messenger, "Why have those Messengers taken these cords and gone off?"

He said to me, "They have gone to measure."

³Then the Messenger who went with me said to me,

> "These will bring the measures of the right-doers, and the ropes of the right-doers to the right-doers, that they may secure themselves with stays on the name of the Lord of Spirits forever and ever. ⁴The elect will begin to dwell with the elect, and those are the measures which will be given to faith and which will strengthen righteousness.

> ⁵"These measures will reveal all the secrets of the depths of the earth, and those who have been destroyed by the desert, and those who have been devoured by the beasts, and those who have been devoured by the fish of the sea, that they may return and secure themselves with stays on the day of the Elect One.

> "For none will be destroyed before the Lord of Spirits, and none can be destroyed. ⁶All who dwell above in the heaven received a command and power and one voice and one light like fire. ⁷And that One, with their first words they blessed, extolled, and praised with wisdom. They were wise in utterance and in the spirit of life.

> ⁸"The Lord of Spirits placed the Elect One on the throne of glory [esteem], and He will judge all the works of the set-apart above in the heaven, and in the balance their deeds will be weighed

> ⁹"When He will lift up his face to judge their secret ways according to the word of the name of the Lord of Spirits and their path according to the way of the righ-

teous judgment of the Lord of Spirits, then they all with one voice will speak, bless, glorify, extol, and sanctify [set-apart] the name of the Lord of Spirits.

10"He will summon all the armies of the heavens, all the set-apart ones above, the armies of Elahim, the Cherubim, Seraphim and Ophannim, all the Messengers of power, all the Messengers of principalities, the Elect One, and the other powers on the earth and over the water. 11On that day they will raise one voice, and bless, glorify, and exalt in the spirit of faith, in the spirit of wisdom, in the spirit of patience, in the spirit of mercy, in the spirit of judgment and of peace, in the spirit of goodness, and all will say with one voice,

'Blessed is He and may the name of the Lord of Spirits be blessed for ever and ever. 12All who do not sleep above in heaven bless Him. All the set-apart ones who are in heaven bless Him. All the elect who dwell in the garden of life, and every spirit of light who is able to bless glorify, extol, and hallow Your blessed name. And all flesh will beyond measure glorify and bless your name forever and ever. 13For great is the mercy of the Lord of Spirits. He is long-suffering. All His works and all that He has created He has revealed to the righteous and elect in the name of the Lord of Spirits.' "

CHAPTER 62

The Lord commanded the kings, the mighty, the exalted, and those who dwell on the earth, and said,

"Open your eyes and lift up your horns if you are able
to recognize the Elect [Chosen] One."

2The Lord of Spirits seated Him on the throne of His glory [esteem], and the spirit of righteousness was poured out upon Him, and the word of his mouth slays all the wrong doers, and all the unrighteous are destroyed from before His face."

3All the kings and the mighty there will stand up in that day with the exalted, and those who hold the earth. They will see and recognize how He sits on the throne of His glory, how righteousness is judged before him, and how no lying word is spoken before him.

⁴Then pain will come on them, like on a woman in travail when in giving birth her child enters the mouth of the womb causing pain. ⁵One portion of them will look on the other, and they will be terrified. They will be downcast of countenance, and pain will seize them when they see the Son of Man Sitting on the throne of his glory.

⁶The kings, the mighty, and all who possess the earth will bless, glorify, and honor Him who rules over all, and who was hidden.

⁷For from the beginning the Son of Man was hidden, and the Most High preserved Him in the presence of His might and revealed him to the elect. ⁸The congregation of the elect and set-apart will be sown. All the elect will stand before Him on that day.

⁹All the kings, the mighty, the exalted, and those who rule the earth shall fall down before him on their faces, and worship and set their hope upon that Son of Man, and petition and supplicate Him for mercy at his hands. ¹⁰Nevertheless the Lord of Spirits will so press them that they will quickly go away from His presence. Their faces will be filled with shame, and darkness will grow deeper on their faces.

¹¹He will deliver them to the Messengers for punishment, to execute vengeance on them because they oppressed His children and His elect. ¹²They will be a spectacle for the right-doers and for His elect, and they will rejoice over them, because the wrath of the Lord of Spirits rests upon them, and His sword is drunk with their blood.

¹³The righteous and elect will be saved on that day, and from that day on they will never see the face of the doers of wrong and unrighteous. ¹⁴The Lord of Spirits will abide over them, and with the Son of Man shall they eat, lie down, and rise up forever and ever. ¹⁵The righteous and elect will have risen from the earth, and ceased to be of downcast countenance. ¹⁶They will have been clothed with garments of glory [esteem], and these will be the garments of life from the Lord of Spirits,

"And your garments will not grow old, nor your glory
[esteem] pass away before the Lord of Spirits."

CHAPTER 63

In those days the mighty and the kings who possess the earth will implore Him to grant them a little rest from His Messengers of punishment to whom they were delivered, that they might fall down and worship before the Lord of Spirits, and confess their wrong doings before Him. ²And they will bless and glorify the Lord of Spirits, and say,

> "Blessed is the Lord of Spirits and the Lord of kings,
> and the Lord of the mighty and the Lord of the rich, and
> the Lord of glory and the Lord of wisdom, ³and splendid
> in every secret thing is Your power from generation to
> generation, And Your glory forever and ever. Deep are all
> Your secrets and innumerable, and Your righteousness is
> beyond reckoning. ⁴We have now learned that we should
> glorify and bless the Lord of kings and Him who is king
> over all kings."

⁵They will say,

> "We desire that we had rest to glorify, give thanks, and
> confess our faith before His glory! ⁶Now we long for a little
> rest but we do not find it. We follow hard upon it but we
> do not receive it. Light has vanished from before us, and
> darkness is our dwelling place forever and ever. ⁷For we
> have not believed Him nor glorified the name of the Lord
> of Spirits, nor glorified our Lord. But our hope was in the
> scepter of *our* kingdom, and in *our* glory. ⁸But in the day
> of our suffering and tribulation He does not save, and we
> find no reprieve for [our] confession that our Lord is true
> in all His works, His judgments, and His justice. His judg-
> ments have no respect of persons. ⁹And we pass away
> from before His face on account of our works, and all our
> wrong doings are reckoned up in righteousness."

¹⁰Now they will say to themselves,

> "Our souls are full of unrighteous gain, but that gain
> does not prevent us from descending from the midst of it
> into the burden of Sheol [the grave]."

¹¹After that their faces will be filled with darkness and shame before

that Son of Man. They will be driven from his presence, and the sword shall remain before His face in their midst.
¹²Thus speaks the Lord of Spirits,

> "This is the ordinance and judgment with respect to the mighty, the kings, the exalted, and those who possess the earth before the Lord of Spirits."

CHAPTER 64

And I saw other forms hidden in that place. ²I heard the voice of the Messenger saying: "These are the Messengers who descended to the earth, and revealed what was hidden to the children of men, and seduced the children of men into committing great errors."

CHAPTER 65 [BEGINNING OF A FRAGMENT FROM NOAH]

In those days Noah saw that the earth had sunk down [inclined] and its destruction was near. ²And he arose and went from there to the ends of the earth, and cried aloud to his grandfather Enoch. Noah said three times with an embittered voice,

> "Hear me, hear me, hear me. ³Tell me what it is that is *falling out on the earth* that the earth is in such evil plight *[glowing] and shaken*, lest by some chance I will perish with it *[the impact]*?"

⁴Upon that there was a great commotion [pertubation] on the earth, and a voice was heard from heaven, and I [Noah] fell on my face. ⁵And Enoch my grandfather came and stood by me, and said to me,

> "Why have you cried to me with a bitter cry and weeping? ⁶A command has gone forth from the presence of the Lord concerning those who dwell on the earth that their ruin is accomplished [doom has arrived], because they have learned all the secrets of the Messengers, all the violence of the adversaries, all their powers including the most secret ones, all the power of those who practice sorcery, the power of witchcraft, and the power of those who make molten images for the whole earth and ⁷how silver is produced from the dust of the earth, and how soft metal

originates in the earth. [8]For lead and tin are not produced from the earth like the first. It is a fountain [volcanism?] that produces them, and a Messenger stands in it, and that Messenger has the authority over it."

[9]And after that my grandfather Enoch took hold of me by my hand and raised me up, and said to me,

"Go, for I have asked the Lord of Spirits as touching this commotion [pertubation] on the earth. [10]And He said to me, 'Because of their unrighteousness, their judgment has been determined upon [them] and shall not be withheld by Me for ever. Because of the sorceries, which they searched out and learned, the earth and those who dwell upon it will be destroyed.'

[11]"And these have no place of repentance forever because they have shown to the people what was hidden, and they are the damned. But as for you, my son, the Lord of Spirits knows that you are pure and guiltless of this reproach concerning the secrets.

[12]And He has destined your name to be among the set-apart and will preserve you from among those who dwell on the earth and has destined your righteous seed both for kingship and for great honors. From your seed will proceed the fountain of the righteous and the set-apart without number for ever."

CHAPTER 66

After that he showed me the Messengers of punishment who are prepared to come and let loose all the powers of the waters which are beneath in the earth in order to bring judgment and destruction on all who live on the earth. [2]And the Lord of Spirits gave commandment to the Messengers who were going forth that they should not cause the waters to rise but should hold them in check for those Messengers were over the powers of the waters. [3]And I went away from the presence of Enoch.

CHAPTER 67

In those days the word of God came to me. He said:

"Noah, your lot has come up before Me, a lot without blame, a lot of love and uprightness. ²Now the Messengers are making a wooden building [ark], and when they have completed that task, I will place My hand upon it and preserve it, and there will come forth from it the seed of life. A change will set in so that the earth will not remain without inhabitant. ³I will make fast your seed before me forever and ever, and I will spread abroad those [creatures] who live with you. They will not be unfruitful on the face of the earth, but they will be blessed and multiply on the earth in the name of the Lord."

⁴He will imprison those Messengers, who have shown unrighteousness, in that burning valley which my grandfather Enoch had formerly shown to me in the west among the mountains of gold, silver, iron, soft metal, and tin.

⁵I saw that valley in which there was a great violent disturbance and a convulsion of the waters. ⁶When all this took place, from that fiery molten metal and from the convulsion in that place, there was produced a smell of sulfur, and it was connected with those waters. In that valley, the Messengers who had led astray Mankind, burned beneath that land.

⁷Through its valleys proceed streams of fire, where these Messengers are punished who led astray those who dwell upon the earth. ⁸But those waters shall in those days serve for the kings and the mighty and the exalted, and those who dwell on the earth, for the healing of the body, but for the punishment of the spirit; now their spirit is full of lust, that they may be punished in their body, for they have denied the Lord of Spirits and see their punishment daily, and yet do not believe in His name.

⁹In proportion as the burning of their bodies becomes severe, a corresponding change shall take place in their spirit forever and ever. For before the Lord of Spirits none will utter an idle word. ¹⁰For the judgment shall come on them because they believe in the lust of their body and deny the Spirit of the Lord.

¹¹Those same waters will undergo a change in those days. For when

those Messengers are punished in these waters, these water-springs will change their temperature, and when the Messengers ascend, this water of the springs will change and become cold.

¹²And I heard Michael answering:

> This judgment, with which the Messengers are judged, is a testimony for the kings and the mighty who possess the earth.

> ¹³Because these waters of judgment minister to the healing of the body of the kings and the lust of their body; therefore they will not see and will not believe that those waters will change and become a fire which burns for ever.

CHAPTER 68

After that my grandfather Enoch gave me the teaching of all the secrets in the book in the Parables which had been given to him, and he put them together for me in the words of the **Book of the Parables**.

²On that day Michael answered Raphael and said:

> "The power of the spirit transports and makes me tremble because of the severity of the judgment of the secrets, and the judgment of the Messengers. Who can endure the severe judgment which has been executed, and before which they melt away?"

³Michael answered again, and said to Raphael,

> "Who is he whose heart is not softened concerning it, and whose reins are not troubled by this word of judgment that has gone forth upon them because of those who have thus led them out?"

⁴It came to pass, when he stood before the Lord of Spirits, Michael said to Raphael,

> "I will not take their part under the eye of the Lord for the Lord of Spirits has been angry with them because they do as if they were the Lord. ⁵Therefore all that is hidden will come upon them forever and ever; for neither Messenger nor man will have his portion in it, but alone they

have received their judgment forever and ever."

CHAPTER 69

After this judgment they shall terrify and make them tremble because they have shown this to those who dwell on the earth. ²Here are the names of those Messengers:

- The first of them is Samjaza,
- the second Artaqifa,
- and the third Armen,
- the fourth Kokabel,
- the fifth Turael,
- the sixth Rumjal,
- the seventh Danjal,
- the eighth Neqael,
- the ninth Baraqel,
- the tenth Azazel,
- the eleventh Armaros,
- the twelfth Batarjal,
- the thirteenth Busasejal,
- the fourteenth Hananel,
- the fifteenth Turel,
- and the sixteenth Simapesiel,
- the seventeenth Jetrel,
- the eighteenth Tumael,
- the nineteenth Turel,
- the twentieth Rumael,
- the twenty-first Azazel.

³These are the chiefs of their Messengers and their names, and their chief ones over hundreds and over fifties and over tens.

⁴• The name of the first Jeqon: that is, the one who led astray all the sons of God, and brought them down to the earth, and led them astray through the daughters of men.

⁵• The second was named Asbeel: he imparted to the set-apart sons of God evil counsel, and led them astray so

that they defiled their bodies with the daughters of men.

⁶• The third was named Gadreel: he it is who showed the children of men all the blows of death, and he led astray Eve, and showed (the weapons of death to the sons of men) the shield and the coat of mail, and the sword for battle, and all the weapons of death to the children of men. ⁷And from his hand they have proceeded against those who dwell on the earth from that day and for evermore.

⁸• The fourth was named Penemue: he taught the children of men the bitter and the sweet, and he taught them all the secrets of their wisdom. ⁹And he instructed mankind in writing with ink and paper, and thereby many sinned from eternity to eternity and until this day. ¹⁰For men were not created for such a purpose, to give confirmation to their good faith with pen and ink. ¹¹For men were created exactly like the Messengers, to the intent that they should continue pure and righteous, and death, which destroys everything, could not have taken hold of them, but through this their knowledge they are perishing, and through this power it is consuming me.

¹²• The fifth was named Kasdeja: this is he who showed the children of men all the wicked smiting of spirits and demons, and the smiting of the embryo in the womb, that it may pass away, and the smiting of the soul the bites of the serpent, and the smiting which befall through the noontide heat, the son of the serpent named Taba'et.

¹³This is the task of Kasbeel, the chief of the oath, which he showed to the set-apart ones when he dwelt high above in glory, and its name is Biqa. ¹⁴This Messenger requested Michael to show him the hidden name that he might enunciate it in the oath so that those who revealed all that was in secret to the children of men might quake before that name and oath. ¹⁵This is the power of this oath for it is powerful and strong, and he placed this oath [named] Akae in the hand of Michael.

¹⁶These are the secrets of this oath and they are strong through his oath.

The heaven was suspended before the world was created and forever. [17]Through it the earth was founded upon the water, and from the secret recesses of the mountains come beautiful waters, from the creation of the world and to eternity. [18]Through that oath the sea was created, and as its foundation he set for it the sand against the time of its anger, and it dare not pass beyond it from the creation of the world unto eternity.

[19]Through that oath are the depths made fast and abide and stir not from their place from eternity to eternity. [20]Through that oath the sun and moon complete their course, and deviate not from their ordinance from eternity to eternity. [21]Through that oath the stars complete their course, and He calls them by their names, and they answer Him from eternity to eternity.

[22]In like manner [came] the spirits of the water, of the winds, of all zephyrs, and their paths from all the quarters of the winds. [23]In them are preserved the voices of the thunder and the light of the lightning, and [in] there are preserved the chambers of the hail, the chambers of the hoar-frost, the chambers of the mist, the chambers of the rain, and the dew.

[24]All these believe and give thanks before the Lord of Spirits, and glorify Him with all their power, and their food is in every act of thanksgiving. They thank and glorify and extol the name of the Lord of Spirits forever and ever. [25]And this oath is mighty over them and through it they are preserved, and their paths are preserved, and their course is not destroyed.

[26]There was great joy among them, and they blessed and glorified and extolled because the name of that Son of Man had been revealed to them. [27]He sat on the throne of His glory, and the sum of judgment was given to the Son of Man, and he caused the sinners to pass away and be destroyed from off the face of the earth. [28]With chains will those who led the world astray be bound. They will be imprisoned in their assembly place of destruction, and all their works will vanish from the face of the earth.

[29]From that time on there will be nothing corruptible, for that Son of Man has appeared and has seated Himself on the throne of His glory. All evil will pass away before his face. The word of that Son of Man will go forth and be strong before the Lord of Spirits.

This completes the *third parable* of Enoch.

CHAPTER 70

It came to pass after this that his [Enoch's] name during his lifetime was raised aloft to that Son of Man and to the Lord of Spirits from among those who dwell on the earth. ²And he was raised aloft on the chariots of the spirit and his name vanished among them. ³From that day I was no longer numbered among them, and he set me between the two winds, between the North and the West, where the Messengers took the cords to measure for me the place for the elect and righteous. ⁴There I saw the first fathers and the doers of right who from the beginning dwell in that place.

CHAPTER 71

After this my spirit was translated and it ascended into the heavens. And I saw the set-apart sons of God. They were stepping on flames of fire, and their garments were white and [also] their raiment, and their faces shone like snow.

²I saw two streams of fire, and the light of that fire shone like hyacinth. And I fell on my face before the Lord of Spirits. ³The Messenger Michael, one of the Arch-messengers, seized me by my right hand and lifted me up and led me forth into all the secrets. ⁴He showed me all the secrets of righteousness, all the secrets of the ends of the heaven, and all the chambers of all the stars and all the luminaries from where they proceed before the face of the set-apart ones.

⁵And he translated my spirit into the heaven of heavens, and I saw there as it were a structure built of crystals and between those crystals [I saw] tongues of living fire. ⁶My spirit saw the girdle, which circled that house of fire. On its four sides were streams full of living fire, and they circled that house. ⁷Round about were Seraphim, Cherubim, and Ophannim. These are they who do not sleep, and who guard the throne of His glory.

⁸I saw Messengers who could not be counted, a thousand thousand, and ten thousand times ten thousand, encircling that house.

Michael, Raphael, Gabriel, Phanuel, and the set-apart Messengers, who are above the heavens, go in and out of that house. ⁹They came out from that house, Michael, Gabriel, Raphael, Phanuel, and many set-apart Messengers without number. ¹⁰With them was the Head of Days. His head white and pure as wool, and His raiment indescribable. ¹¹And I fell on my face, and my whole body became relaxed, and my spirit was transfigured. And I cried with a loud voice with the spirit of power, and blessed, glorified, and extolled.

[12]And these blessings, which went forth out of my mouth, were well pleasing before that Head of Days. [13]And the Head of Days came with Michael, Gabriel, Raphael, Phanuel, and thousands and ten thousands of Messengers without number. [14]And a [Messenger] came to me and greeted me with his voice and said to me,

> "This is the Son of Man who is born in righteousness, and righteousness abides over Him, and the righteousness of the Head of Days does not leave Him.
>
> [15]"He proclaims to you peace in the name of the world to come. For from hence has proceeded peace since the creation of the world. So will it be to you forever and forever and ever.
>
> [16]"All will walk in His ways because righteousness never leaves Him. With Him will be their dwelling places, and with him their heritage. They will not be separated from him forever and ever and ever. [17]There will be length of days with that Son of Man, and the righteous will have peace and an upright way in the name of the Lord of Spirits forever and ever."

The Book of the Courses
of the Luminaries

⧗

I n the first two books we see a picture of life on earth that may seem too simple for our *civilized* minds. Enoch writes with some wonder and awe about the changes in the climate, about the lightning and thunder, the leaves changing and falling from the trees, the changes in the wind including its force and direction, about how the plants emerge from the earth only to die again after the summer heat, and many more observations.

But there was one thing missing: the knowledge about the precision of the relationship between the earth, the moon, the sun and the stars. Left to his own devices, Enoch may have tried to record the passing of days and seasons, but apparently nothing more.

Then a Messenger from the heavens came to him with the exact purpose of giving to Enoch the knowledge he missed. These were called by Uriel, the Laws of the luminaries and how they would exists until the new heavens and the new earth was created – something we may have thought was only a New Testament idea.

The calendar revealed to Enoch is only a solar calendar with no adjustments on account of lunar events. The calendar starts on the day in spring when the night and day are equal. Each day was divided into 18 parts. So in the spring the first day had nine light parts and nine dark parts. This is also called an *equinox*, although that word does not appear in Enoch's writings. A similar solar event happened in the fall. The other two quarters started on solstices. In the summer this is the day when the light part of the day reaches its maximum duration when compared to the dark time. The opposite happens in the winter. This also shows that Enoch was located north of the equator. Each quarter of the year starts on a solar event: spring equinox, summer solstice, fall equinox, winter solstice.

Unlike our calendars this one always started on the fourth day of the week, and had quarters of equal length of 91 days, which is the same as 13 weeks. The beginning and end of a day was always at sunset.

The solar events mentioned above and the sunsets made it possible to know the time of the year and the day by observation only – something we don't do today.

This makes it possible for us to also know where we are in time, regardless of the political or religious calendar currently in vogue.

The prophet Daniel later wrote about those who would "*think* to change the times and the seasons." They could not destroy the calendar revealed to Enoch because to do so, they would have had to knock the earth out of its orbit, which no doubt would have destroyed all life anyway.

Something did happen to the earth. Before the flood a large supply of water existed above the troposphere, where our weather exists. Above the troposphere is the stratosphere where the ozone layer is found. Before the great flood, it contained the "waters above."

Up until the mid to late 1930s it was believed that the rotation speed of the earth was an unchanging constant. However, that was found to be false. The rotation speed of the earth is in constant flux. Storms and large movements of water as in tsunamis cause the earth's rotation to speed up or slow down. The "waters above" acted like a spinning ice skater's arms. When held out the spin slows, and when drawn in, the spin speeds up. A change in earth's rotation isn't noticed by us. But it has to be taken into account by NASA when calculating trajectories for space exploration.

During the flood, the "waters above" came down, and like the skater drawing her arms in close to her body, the earth's rotation increased fast enough to cause an extra 1.242 days to be added to the solar year. That amounts to an increase in speed of about 5 feet per second.

Enoch also received information about the moon and the lunar year. He showed it to be shorter than the solar year by 10 days. This provides another clue about that happened during the flood. Now the difference between the number of days in a solar year and a lunar year is about 11 days. If the number of days in a lunar year increased by about one day and the number of days in the solar year also increased by about the same amount, the common factor affecting both counts was the rotation speed of the earth. That the lunar year is slightly less than 1.242 days is due to the drag of the earth's gravity on the moon causing the moon's orbital speed to increase slightly over time.

How can we account for the extra 1.242 days and still keep in sync with the revealed calendar? The extra day was a result of great corruption and rebellion on the earth. If it wasn't for the flood all life on the earth was headed for extinction, not unlike where we are now in world affairs. The extra day could be considered by Scripture as a cursed day. A day that exists "without a home."

Various ways have been attempt to keep a "360" year. Most ideas were in violation of the "Laws" given to Enoch by Uriel. This included the extra day at the end of each quarter where the third month of each quarter has 31 days. The extra day added at the end of the third month is not counted, which means it is an intercalary day. This is hard to understand because we count every last second.

But, for the purpose of keeping track of the times and seasons, and later the Festivals and High Days, and the prophecies associated with them, only 360 of the 364 days are "counted." For this reason in Scripture 1,260 days is the same as 42 months, and the same as three and one-half years.

To preserve the revealed structure, we must keep the calendar intact according to the revelation and not "mess with it" in an attempt to make it "convenient" for us! We must understand that the actual length of Enoch's year is a constant. The time between spring equinoxes and fall equinoxes is the same now as it was then. But we must not allow the counting of days to confuse us. The number of days did change, but the length of the year in hours or minutes did not.

There is a Jewish tradition of two starting points for the year. One was called the *sacred year*, the other the *civil year*. There is also a tradition of starting the year by *observation*. But instead of observing the equinoxes, the Jews started to look for the new moon – a mistake according to Enoch and the Book of Jubilees.

The Torah gives us a clue. There are two Feast and High Day seasons in the year - the *early* and the *latter*. The early starts on the first day of the first month. The latter starts on the first day of the seventh month. Why was Moses given this Law? Because these are the two equinoxes of the year. This is also the source of the *dual year* tradition.

REPEATING CYCLES FOR THE QUARTERS:

MONTHS **1**, 4, **7**, 10

			1 SE	2	3	4
5	6	7	8	9	10	11
12	13	14	15	16	17	18
19	20	21	22	23	24	25
26	27	28	29	30		

MONTHS 2, 5, 8, 11

					1	2
3	4	5	6	7	8	9
10	11	12	13	14	15	16
17	18	29	20	21	22	23
24	25	26	27	28	29	30

MONTHS 3, 6, 9, 12

1	2	3	4	5	6	7
8	9	10	11	12	13	14
15	16	17	18	19	20	21
22	23	24	25	26	27	28
29	30	31				

SE is Solar Event: Months 1, 7 the Equinoxes; 4, 10 the Solstices. 31 is intercalary day.

Even though we now have a faster day, these two times allow us to reset relative to the two equinoxes so that we can keep the Feasts, High Days, and weekly Sabbaths on the *clean* days. After *observing* these two solar events we can count days, even though they are five minutes shorter now. But the result is that the real time from year to year is preserved as a constant. There is no need to tack on an extra day at the end of each year. We simply wait for the equinox twice per year and restart the counting. When combined with observing days from sunset to sunset, the process takes care of the five minute per day shortfall.

No *real* time was added to the length of the year revealed to Enoch, but the flood caused an increase in the rotation speed that resulted in a change in the number of days in the year. However, the *elapsed time* in minutes or hours of the year is a constant. The number of days is not. The *restoration* will include the slowing of the earth's rotation!

The Book of the *Luminaries* is another Key to Scriptures that has been maligned and intentionally squelched. But its message is laced throughout all the Scriptures and cannot be removed from it. Without Enoch, we would understand nothing about our future.

THE BOOK OF THE COURSES OF THE LUMINARIES

CHAPTER 72

The book of the courses of the luminaries [sun and moon] of the heaven, the relations of each, according to their classes, their dominion and their seasons, according to their names and places of origin, and according to their months.

Uriel, the set-apart Messenger, who was with me, who is their guide, *showed me all their laws exactly as they are, and how it is with regard to all the years of the world and unto eternity, until the new creation is accomplished which endures until eternity.*

²This is the first law of the luminaries.

The luminary, the Sun, has its rising in the eastern gates of the heaven, and its setting in the western gates of the heaven. ³And I saw six gates in which the sun rises, and six gates in which the sun sets. The moon also rises and sets in these gates.

The leaders of the stars and those whom they lead, six in the east and six in the west, all follow each other in accurate corresponding order. There are also many windows to the right and left of these gates.

⁴And first goes the great luminary, the Sun, and his circumference [path] is like the circumference of the heaven. The sun is filled with il-luminating and heating fire. ⁵The chariot on which he ascends, the wind drives, and the sun goes down from the heaven and returns through the

north in order to reach the east, and is so guided that he comes to the that gate and shines in the face of the heaven.

The Spring Equinox

[6]In this way he rises in the first month in the great gate, which is the fourth of those six gates in the east.

[7]And in that fourth gate from which the sun rises in the first month are twelve window openings from which a flame advances when they are opened in their season.

[8]When the sun rises in the heaven, he comes through that fourth gate thirty mornings in succession and sets accurately in the fourth gate in the west of the heaven. [9]During this period the day becomes longer and the night shorter to the thirtieth morning.

[10]On that day the day is longer than the night by a ninth part. The day amounts exactly to ten parts and the night to eight parts. [11]The sun rises from that fourth gate, and sets in the fourth.

After that the sun returns to the fifth gate of the east thirty mornings, and rises from it and sets in the fifth gate. [12]Then the day becomes longer by two parts and amounts to eleven parts, and the night becomes shorter and amounts to seven parts.

[13]Then it returns to the east and enters into the sixth gate and rises and sets in the sixth gate thirty-one mornings on account of its sign.

The Summer Solstice

[14]On that day the day becomes longer than the night, and the day becomes double the night. The day becomes twelve parts, and the night is shortened and becomes six parts.

[15]And the sun mounts up to make the day shorter and the night longer, and the sun returns to the east and enters into the sixth gate, and rises from it and sets thirty mornings.

[16]And when thirty mornings are accomplished, the day decreases by exactly one part, and becomes eleven parts, and the night seven.

[17]And the sun goes out from that sixth gate in the west, and goes to the east and rises in the fifth gate for thirty mornings, and sets in the west again in the fifth western gate.

¹⁸On that day the day decreases by two parts, and amounts to ten parts and the night to eight parts. ¹⁹And the sun goes out from that fifth gate and sets in the fifth gate of the west, and rises in the fourth gate for thirty-one mornings on account of its sign, and sets in the west.

Autumnal Equinox

²⁰On that day the day is equalized with the night, and becomes of equal length, and the night amounts to nine parts and the day to nine parts. ²¹And the sun rises from that gate and sets in the west, and returns to the east and rises thirty mornings in the third gate and sets in the west in the third gate. ²²On that day the night becomes longer than the day, and night becomes longer than the [previous] night, and day shorter than [the previous] day until the thirtieth morning, and the night amounts exactly to ten parts and the day to eight parts.

²³And the sun rises from that third gate and sets in the third gate in the west and returns to the east, and for thirty mornings rises in the second gate in the east, and in like manner sets in the second gate in the west of the heaven. ²⁴On that day the night amounts to eleven parts and the day to seven parts.

²⁵And the sun rises on that day from that second gate and sets in the west in the second gate, and returns to the east into the first gate for thirty-one mornings, and sets in the first gate in the west of the heaven.

The Winter Solstice

²⁶On that day the night becomes longer and amounts to the double of the day and the night amounts exactly to twelve parts and the day to six. ²⁷And the sun has now traversed the divisions of his orbit and turns again on those divisions of his orbit, and enters that gate thirty mornings and sets also in the west opposite to it.

²⁸And on that night has the night decreased in length by a ninth part, and the night has become eleven parts and the day seven parts. ²⁹And the sun has returned and entered into the second gate in the east, and returns on those his divisions of his orbit for thirty mornings, rising and setting. ³⁰And on that day the night decreases in length, and the night amounts to ten parts and the day to eight.

³¹And on that day the sun rises from that gate, and sets in the west, and returns to the east, and rises in the third gate for thirty-one mornings, and sets in the west of the heaven.

Spring Equinox

³²On that day the night decreases and amounts to nine parts, and the day to nine parts. The night is equal to the day. At that time the year is exactly three hundred and sixty-four days.

³³The length of the day and of the night and the shortness of the day and of the night, arise through the course of the sun and [from] these distinctions [the quarters] are separated. ³⁴So [as at the beginning] the year comes back to its course where the day becomes longer, and each night becomes shorter.

³⁵This is the law and the course of the sun. Its return, as often as it returns and rises [three-hundred?] sixty times, the great luminary named the sun, [is] forever and ever. ³⁶And that which thus rises is the [same] great luminary, and is so named [the sun] according to its appearance, as the Lord commanded.

³⁷As it rises, so it sets and decreases not, and rests not, but runs day and night. Its light is sevenfold brighter than that of the moon. As regards size, they [appear] equal.

CHAPTER 73

And after this law I saw another law dealing with the smaller luminary, which is named the Moon. ²Her circumference [orbit] is like the circumference of the heaven. Her chariot in which she rides is driven by the wind, and light is given to her in definite measure.

³Her rising and setting change every month. Her days are like the days of the sun, and when her light is uniform [full] it amounts to the seventh part of the light of the sun. ⁴And thus she rises. Her first phase in the east comes forth on the thirtieth morning. On that day she becomes visible, and constitutes for you the first phase of the moon on the thirtieth day together with the sun in the gate where the sun rises. ⁵And the one half of her goes forth by a seventh part, and her whole circumference [orbit] is empty, wiyout light, with the exception of one-seventh part of it, and

the fourteenth part of her light. ⁶And when she receives one-seventh part of the half of her light, her light amounts to one-seventh part and the half thereof.

⁷She sets with the sun, and when the sun rises the moon rises with him and receives the half of one part of light, and in that night in the beginning of her morning in the commencement of the lunar day the moon sets with the sun, and is invisible that night with the fourteen parts and the half of one of them. ⁸She rises on that day with exactly a seventh part, and comes forth and recedes from the rising of the sun, and in her remaining days she becomes bright in the remaining thirteen parts.

CHAPTER 74

And I saw another course, a law for her, and how according to that law she performs her monthly revolution. ²And all these Uriel, the set-apart Messenger who is the leader of them all, showed to me, and their positions, and I wrote down their positions as he showed them to me, and I wrote down their months as they were, and the appearance of their lights until fifteen days were accomplished.

³In single seventh parts she accomplishes all her light in the east, and in single seventh parts accomplishes all her darkness in the west. ⁴And in certain months she alters her settings, and in certain months she pursues her own peculiar course.

⁵In two months the moon sets with the sun. In those two middle gates the third and the fourth. ⁶She goes forth for seven days, and turns about and returns again through the gate where the sun rises, and accomplishes all her light: and she recedes from the sun, and in eight days enters the sixth gate from which the sun goes forth. ⁷And when the sun goes forth from the fourth gate she goes forth seven days, until she goes forth from the fifth, and turns back again in seven days into the fourth gate and accomplishes all her light. And she recedes and enters into the first gate in eight days. ⁸And she returns again in seven days into the fourth gate from which the sun goes forth. ⁹Thus I saw their position – how the moons rose and the sun set in those days.

¹⁰If five years are added together the sun has a surplus of thirty days, and all the days that accrue to it for one of those five years, when they are full,

amount to 364 days. ¹¹And the surplus of the sun and of the stars amounts to six days. In five years, six days [for] every year comes to 30 days, and the moon falls behind the sun and stars to the number of 30 days.

> [That paragraph appears to be in reference to lunar year calcula-
> tion of 354 days compared to solar year of 360 days and not counting
> the intercalary days that fall on the end of each quarter. More simply it
> states that after five years a month of 30 days would need to be includ-
> ed in a lunar year to bring it in line with the solar year when counting
> 360 days. This is the last we hear of this. Ed.]

¹²The sun and the stars bring in all the years exactly, so that they do not advance or delay their position by a single day unto eternity, but complete the years with perfect justice in 364 days.

¹³In three [solar] years there are 1,092 days [3 times 364], and in five years 1,820 days [5 times 364], and in eight years there are 2,912 days [8 times 364].

¹⁴But for the moon alone the days in 3 years amount to 1,062 days [1092 – 30]. And in 5 years she falls 50 days behind. ¹⁵ And in 5 years there are 1,770 days [1820 – 50].

¹⁶And for the moon the days in 8 years amount to 2,832 days [2912 – 80]; for in 8 years she falls behind to the amount of 80 days, all the days she falls behind in 8 years are 80.

> [After the flood, this no longer applies as the earth now rotated
> faster, and the difference between the lunar year and solar year is now
> about 11 days. Ed.]

¹⁷And the year is accurately completed in conformity with their world-stations and the stations of the sun, which rise from the gates through which it the sun rises and sets 30 days.

CHAPTER 75

And the leaders of the heads of the thousands, who are placed over the whole creation and over all the stars, have also to do with the four interca-lary days, being inseparable from their office. According to the reckoning of the year, these render service on the four days, which are not counted in the calculation of the year.

²On account of these men go wrong, for those luminaries truly render

service on the world-stations, one in the first gate, one in the third gate of the heaven, one in the fourth gate, and one in the sixth gate, and the exactness of the year is accomplished through its separate three hundred and sixty-four stations.

3For the signs, the times, the years, and the days, the Messenger Uriel showed to me, whom the Lord of glory set for ever over all the luminaries of the heaven, in the heaven and in the world that they should rule on the face of the heaven and be seen on the earth, and be leaders for the day and the night, i.e. the sun, moon, and stars, and all the ministering creatures which make their revolution in all the chariots of the heaven.

4In like manner the twelve gates Uriel showed me open in the circumference of the sun's chariot in the heaven, through which the rays of the sun break forth. From them warmth is diffused over the earth, when they are opened at their appointed seasons, 5and for the winds and the spirit of the dew when they are opened, standing open in the heavens at the ends.

6As for the twelve gates in the heaven, at the ends of the earth, out of which go forth the sun, moon, and stars, and all the works of heaven in the east and in the west. 7There are many windows open to the left and right of them, and one window at its appointed season produces warmth, corresponding as these do to those gates from which the stars come forth according as He has commanded them, and wherein they set corresponding to their number.

8And I saw chariots in the heaven, running in the world, above those gates in which revolve the stars that never set. 9One is larger than all the rest, and it is that that makes its course through the entire world.

CHAPTER 76

And at the ends of the earth I saw twelve gates open to all the quarters of the heaven, from which the winds go forth and blow over the earth. 2Three of them are open on the face in the east of the heavens, and three in the west, and three on the right in the south of the heaven, and three on the left in the north.

3And the three first are those of the east, and three are of the north, and three after those on the left of the south, and three of the west. 4Through four of these come winds of blessing and prosperity, and from those eight come hurtful winds: when they are sent, they bring destruction on all the earth and on the water upon it, and on all who dwell thereon, and on everything which is in the water and on the land.

⁵And the first wind from those gates, called the east wind, comes through the first gate, which is in the east, inclining towards the south. From it come desolation, drought, heat, and destruction.

⁶And through the second gate in the middle comes what is fitting, and from it comes rain, fruitfulness, prosperity, and dew.

And through the third gate which lies toward the north come cold and drought.

⁷After these come the south winds through three gates. Through the first gate of them inclining to the east comes a hot wind. ⁸Through the middle gate next to it come fragrant smells, dew, rain, prosperity, and health. ⁹And through the third gate lying to the west come dew, rain, locusts and desolation.

¹⁰And after these the north winds: from the seventh gate in the east come dew, rain, locusts and desolation. ¹¹From the middle gate come in a direct direction health and rain and dew and prosperity. And through the third gate in the west come clouds, hoarfrost, snow, rain, dew and locusts.

¹²And after these four are the west winds. Through the first gate adjoining the north come dew, hoarfrost, cold, snow and frost. ¹³And from the middle gate come dew, rain, prosperity and blessing. Through the last gate, which adjoins the south, come drought, desolation, burning and destruction.

¹⁴The twelve gates of the four quarters of the heaven are completed, and all their laws, all their plagues, all their benefactions have I shown to you, my son Methuselah.

CHAPTER 77

And the first quarter is called the east, because it is the first, and the second, the south, *because the Most High will descend there. Yes, there, in quite a special sense, will He who is blessed forever descend.* ²And the west quarter is named the diminished, because there all the luminaries of the heaven wane and go down. ³And the fourth quarter, named the north, is divided into three parts: the first of them is for the dwelling of men; and the second contains seas of water, and the abysses and forests and rivers, and darkness and clouds; and the third part contains the garden of righteousness.

⁴I saw seven high mountains, higher than all the mountains that are on the earth, and thence comes forth hoarfrost, and days, seasons, and years pass away.

⁵I saw seven rivers on the earth larger than all the rivers. One of them, coming from the west, pours its waters into the Great Sea. ⁶And these two come from the north to the sea and pour their waters into the Erythraean Sea in the east. ⁷And the remaining four come forth on the side of the north to their own sea, two of them to the Erythraean Sea, and two into the Great Sea and discharge themselves there and, some say, into the desert.

⁸Seven great islands I saw in the sea and in the mainland. [I saw] two in the mainland and five in the Great Sea.

CHAPTER 78

And the names of the sun are the following: the first Orjares [the diminished sun of the winter?], and the second Tomas [its heat is powerful in the summer?].

²The moon has four names: the first name is Asonja, the second Ebla, the third Benase, and the fourth Erae.

³These are the two great luminaries: their circumference is like the circumference of the heaven, and the size of the circumference of both is alike.

⁴In the circumference of the sun there are seven portions of light, which are added to it more than to the moon, and in definite measures it is transferred until the seventh portion of the sun is exhausted. ⁵And they set and enter the gates of the west, and make their revolution by the north, and come forth through the eastern gates on the face of the heaven.

⁶When the moon rises one-fourteenth part appears in the heaven. The light becomes full in her on the fourteenth [lunar] day she accomplishes her light. ⁷And fifteen parts of light are transferred to her until the fifteenth day when her light is accomplished, according to the sign of the year, and she becomes fifteen parts, and the moon grows by the addition of four-

teenth parts.

⁸In her waning the moon decreases on the first day to fourteen parts of her light, on the second to thirteen parts of light, on the third to twelve, on the fourth to eleven, on the fifth to ten, on the sixth to nine, on the seventh to eight, on the eighth to seven, on the ninth to six, on the tenth to five, on the eleventh to four, on the twelfth to three, on the thirteenth to two, on the fourteenth to the half of a seventh, and all her remaining light disappears wholly on the fifteenth.

⁹And in certain months the [lunar] month has twenty-nine days and once twenty-eight.

¹⁰Uriel showed me another law: when light is transferred to the moon, and on which side the sun transfers it to her. ¹¹During all the period, during which the moon is growing in her light, she is transferring it to herself when opposite to the sun during fourteen days her light is accomplished in the heaven, and when she is illumined throughout, her light is accomplished full in the heaven.

¹²On the first [lunar] day she is called the new moon, for on that day the light rises upon her. ¹³She becomes full moon exactly on the day when the sun sets in the west, and from the east she rises at night, and the moon shines the whole night through until the sun rises over against her and the moon is seen over against the sun. ¹⁴On the side from where the light of the moon comes forth, there again she wanes until all the light vanishes and all the days of the month are at an end, and her circumference is empty, void of light.

¹⁵And three months she makes of thirty days, and at her time she makes three months of twenty- nine days each, in which she accomplishes her waning in the first period of time, and in the first gate for one hundred and seventy-seven days. ¹⁶And in the time of her going out she appears for three months of thirty days each, and for three months she appears of twenty-nine each. ¹⁷At night she appears like a man for twenty days each time, and by day she appears like the heaven, and there is nothing else in her save her light.

CHAPTER 79
And now, my son, I have shown you everything, and the law of all the

stars of the heaven is completed. ²And he showed me all the laws of these for every day, and for every season of bearing rule, and for every year, and for its going forth, and for the order prescribed to it every month and every week.

³And [he showed me] the waning of the moon, which takes place in the sixth gate. For in this sixth gate her light is accomplished, and after that there is the beginning of the waning, ⁴and the waning, which takes place in the first gate in its season, until one hundred and seventy-seven days are accomplished, reckoned according to weeks, twenty-five weeks and two days. ⁵She falls behind the sun and the order of the stars exactly five days in the course of one period, and when this place, which you see, has been traversed. ⁶Such is the picture and sketch of every luminary which Uriel the Archmessenger, who is their leader, showed to me.

CHAPTER 80
And in those days the Messenger Uriel answered and said to me:

"Look, I have shown you everything, Enoch, and I have revealed everything to you that you should see this sun and this moon, and the leaders of the stars of the heaven and all those who turn them, their tasks and times and departures.

²"And in the days of the sinners the years will be shortened, and their seed will be tardy on their lands and fields, and all things on the earth will alter, and will not appear in their time: And the rain will be kept back and the heaven will withhold it.

³"And in those times the fruits of the earth will be backward, and will not grow in their time, and the fruits of the trees will be withheld in their time.

⁴And the moon will alter her order and not appear at her time. [When the rotation of the earth sped up, the orbit speed of the moon also increased due to the gravitational pull of the earth. Ed.]

⁵"And in those days the sun will be seen, and he will journey in the evening on the extremity of the great chariot in the west and shall shine more brightly than accords

with the order of light.

⁶"And many chiefs of the stars will transgress the prescribed order. And these will alter their orbits and tasks and not appear at the seasons prescribed to them.

⁷The whole order of the stars will be concealed from the sinners, and the thoughts of those on the earth will err concerning them, and they will be altered from all their ways. Yes, they will err and take them to be gods.

⁸And evil will be multiplied upon them, and punishment will come upon them so as to destroy all."

CHAPTER 81
And he said to me:

"Observe, Enoch, these heavenly tablets, and read
what is written thereon, and mark every individual fact."

²And I observed the heavenly tablets, and read everything, which was written on them and understood everything, and read the book of all the deeds of mankind, and of all the children of flesh that will be upon the earth to the remotest generations.

³And immediately I blessed the great Lord the King of glory forever, in that He has made all the works of the world, and I extolled the Lord because of His patience, and blessed Him because of the children of men.

⁴After that I said:

"Blessed is the man who dies in righteousness and
goodness, concerning whom there is no book of unrighteousness written, and against whom no day of judgment
will be found."

⁵And those seven holy ones brought me and placed me on the earth before the gate of my house, and said to me:

"Declare everything to your son Methuselah, and
show to all your children that no flesh is righteous in the
sight of the Lord, for He is their Creator. ⁶One year we
will leave you with your son, until you give your last commands, that you may teach your children and record it for
them, and testify to all your children; and in the second

year they will take you from their midst.

⁷Let your heart be strong for the good shall announce righteousness to the good. The righteous with the righteous shall rejoice and shall offer congratulation to one another.

⁸"But the sinners will die with the sinners, and the apostate go down with the apostate. ⁹And those who practice righteousness will die on account of the deeds of men and be taken away on account of the doings of the godless."

¹⁰And in those days they ceased to speak to me, and I came to my people, blessing the Lord of the world.

CHAPTER 82

And now, my son Methuselah, all these things I am recounting to you and writing down for you. I have revealed to you everything and given you books concerning all these. So, my son Methuselah, preserve the books from your father's hand, and see that you deliver them to the generations of the world. ²I have given Wisdom to you and to your children, and your children that will be to you that they may give it to their children for generations, this wisdom namely that passes their thought.

³Those who understand it will not sleep, but will listen with the ear that they may learn this wisdom. And it will please those that eat of it better than good food.

⁴Blessed are all the righteous. Blessed are all those who walk in the way of righteousness and do not as the sinners in the reckoning of all their days in which the sun traverses the heaven entering into and departing from the gates for thirty days with the heads of thousands of the order of the stars, together with the four which are intercalated which divide the four portions of the year, which lead them and enter with them four days.

⁵Owing to them men will be at fault and not reckon them in the whole reckoning of the year. Yes, men will be at fault, and not recognize them accurately. ⁶For they belong to the reckoning of the year and are truly recorded thereon for ever, one in the first gate and one in the third, and one in the fourth and one in the sixth, and the year is completed in three hun-

dred and sixty-four days.

⁷And the account of it is accurate and the recorded reckoning of it exact; for the luminaries, and months and festivals, and years and days, has Uriel shown and revealed to me, to whom the Lord of the whole creation of the world has subjected the host of heaven. ⁸He has power over night and day in the heaven to cause the light to give light to men from the sun, moon, and stars, and all the powers of the heaven, which revolve in their circular chariots. ⁹These are the orders of the stars, which set in their places, and in their seasons, festivals, and months.

¹⁰And these are the names of those who lead them, who watch that they enter at their times, in their orders, in their seasons, in their months, in their periods of dominion, and in their positions.

¹¹Their four leaders who divide the four parts of the year enter first; and after them the twelve leaders of the orders who divide the months; and for the three hundred and sixty days there are heads over thousands who divide the days; and for the four intercalary days there are the leaders which divide the four parts of the year. ¹²These heads over thousands are intercalated between leader and leader, each behind a station, but their leaders make the division.

¹³These are the names of the leaders who divide the four parts of the year that are ordained: Milki'el, Hel'emmelek, and Mel'ejal, and Narel.

¹⁴And the names of those who lead them: Adnar'el, and Ijasusa'el, and 'Elome'el. These three follow the leaders of the orders.

There is one that follows the three leaders of the orders that follow those leaders of stations that divide the four parts of the year.

¹⁵In the beginning of the year Melkejal rises first and rules who is named Tam'aini and sun, and all the days of his dominion while he bears rule are ninety-one days.

¹⁶These are the signs of the days which are to be seen on earth in the days of his dominion: sweat, and heat, and calms, and all the trees bear fruit, and leaves are produced on all the trees, and the harvest of wheat, and the rose-flowers, and all the flowers which come forth in the field, but the trees of the winter season become withered.

¹⁷These are the names of the leaders that are under them: Berka'el, Zelebs'el, and another who is added a head of a thousand, called Hilu-

jaseph: and the days of the dominion of this leader are at an end.

¹⁸The next leader after him is Hel'emmelek, who is named the shining sun, and all the days of his light are ninety-one days. ¹⁹These are the signs of his days on the earth: glowing heat and dryness, and the trees ripen their fruits and produce all their fruits ripe and ready, and the sheep pair and become pregnant, and all the fruits of the earth are gathered in, and everything that is in the fields, and the winepress: these things take place in the days of his dominion.

²⁰These are the names, and the orders, and the leaders of those heads of thousands: Gida'ljal, Ke'el, and He'el, and the name of the head of a thousand which is added to them, Asfa'el: and the days of his dominion are at an end.

The Book of Dream Visions

⌛

We have seen how Enoch's writing contributed powerfully to the good news, to prophecy, and to our understanding of the "spine" present throughout all Scriptures. This Book of Dreams or Dream Visions takes us into a prophetic realm that specifically relates to the foreordained history of humanity.

Enoch's prophecies can be an enigma to "prophecy debunkers." Although there are some so-called *prophets* who need *debunking*, they are not anywhere near being in the same league as Enoch, as we shall see.

There are two dream visions in this book. The first resulted in a conversation Enoch had with his own grandfather concerning the coming of the great flood. Enoch mentioned that he saw this dream, before he had taken and wife and during the time when he was learning to write. In this dream he saw the earth being destroyed. After awaking he told this in detail to his grandfather Mahalalel, who prophesied to Enoch and urged him to prayer that there might be a remnant saved from this destruction, so that life could go on and that the earth not be entirely destroyed.

> O God and Lord and Great King, I implore and cry to
> You to fulfill my prayer *to leave me a posterity* on earth
> and not destroy all the flesh of man. Do not make the
> earth without inhabitant, so that there would be an eter-
> nal destruction.

Such was the life of our righteous father, to whom we owe much.

The second dream, again received before Enoch was married, is about the history of Mankind from the time of Adam to the time of the righteousness and eternal life.

The dream sees all humanity in the metaphor of various animals. And it is from this that both the Law of Clean and Unclean meat, and the Law of the Sacrifices was based.

The difficult part for the "scholars" is trying to pin down Enoch to a time after his prophecies "were fulfilled." We have not come to the end of that time, which lies thousands of years in the future.

I was amazed after first reading this, because it appears that Moses received this from Jethro the Priest of Median and his father-in-law, or from the Egyptian libraries. I tend to think it was the former. I had to conclude that Moses knew what was happening and knew that he had to move on with this task. He saw his life and the lives of those who went before him in this document. So Moses was only doing what he was prophesied to do. As he stood by the sea with the "sheep" and pursued by the "wolves" he knew what was going to happen next.

Moses was the first to quote from Enoch.

When combined with Enoch's vision of the "weeks" in the next book, the evidence becomes insurmountable. It is not possible to place this prophecy at any time in the past, nor can one *safely* conclude that it was recently penned. If we conclude that it is true prophecy and has been fulfilled with accuracy from the time it was written, then we are forced to consider those elements that pertain to us and our near and *certain* future.

The metaphor of the animals shows that the elect or chosen were set apart, in the heavens, to be clean, and that the other nations were unclean. This has more to do with false religions, lack of faith, and the adherence to other gods by the nations than it does with eating the flesh of animals. If that were not true, then the symbols of the "eating of My flesh" and the "drinking of My blood," would lose their power. The point is that the elect and righteous could not survive if they feasted upon the "uncleanness" of the other nations. Instead, elect and righteous can only live by feasting on the "clean" spiritual food given by Eyahuwah.

Also the sacrifices were to be made with only "clean" animals. These do not only and forever apply to "Jesus." The sacrifices represent the blood of the righteous and elect, declared to be so by the Lord of Spirits, and sacrificed on earth because of their "cleanness."

What a tragic mess has been made by the "sheep" when they made a religion out of the Law. Everything in the Law or Torah contains powerful prophecies, knowledge, wisdom, and understanding of a Reality that we know little about.

In our day to day religious lives, we strive to pursue things that are unprofitable for us because we see only the religion and not the reality. The revelations, dreams, and visions given to our father Enoch, and meant for us to know and understand, give us *an insider's view* to what is really happening in heaven and on earth.

This Reality extends into our future. Through Enoch we see what we were intended to be from the beginning of it all – before the heavens and the earth were made!

There are more people on earth now than at any other time in the history of Mankind. And we are, all of us, each and everyone, descended from Enoch as an answer to his prayer.

The second dream vision given to Enoch when he was young, carried him throughout his time on earth to provide for us, for whom he prayed. Have we followed his example? We will, if we learn how he *walked with the Elohim* and *lived the eternal life while he walked this earth.*

That is our calling. That is why we were born. We are the answer to his prayer.

The dream-vision of Enoch takes us to a time yet in the future that requires our thought and focus:

> And I saw until all their generations were transformed,
> and they all became white bulls; and the first among
> them became a lamb, and that lamb became a great animal and had great black horns on its head; and the Lord
> of the sheep rejoiced over it and over all the oxen. And I
> slept in their midst, and I awoke and saw everything.

I added headings to the second dream-vision. These helped me to quickly find those prophecies that applied to known times and events.

The "shepherds" are Messengers who are supposed to watch over the "sheep" and to keep them from being completely devoured by the nations that oppress them. They were first assigned after the House of Israel went into captivity. They continued to "shepherd" in their assigned time, over the "sheep" now and in the future. Then their work will be evaluated and they will be judged according to how successful they were in protecting the "sheep."

As in the past, so now. We will see the work of the "shepherds" in war, famine, weather, economy, health, earthquakes and volcanoes, and tsunami. Consider the history of the House of Israel and the House of Judah after the split during the time of Solomon's son until this day. That should serve as a warning as to what we might expect as this age draws to its appointed close.

This is one of the prophecies that we should know, particularly at this time. Understanding this will drive us to pray and intercede on behalf of the elect, lest they also are destroyed from the earth.

THE BOOK OF DREAM VISIONS

CHAPTER 83

Now, my son Methuselah, I will show you all the visions that I have seen and tell them to you in detail before you. ²Two visions I saw before I took a wife, and the one was quite unlike the other. The first I saw when I was learning to write. The second I saw before I took your mother, when I saw a terrible vision. Regarding them I prayed to the Lord.

³I had lain down in the house of my grandfather Mahalalel, when I saw a vision about how the heaven collapsed, was carried off, and fell to the earth.

⁴When it fell to the earth I saw how the earth was swallowed up in a great abyss. Mountains were piled on mountains, and hills sank down on hills. Tall trees were torn from their roots, hurled down and sunk in the abyss.

⁵Upon seeing this a word fell into my mouth, and I raised my voice to cry aloud, "The earth is destroyed."

⁶My grandfather Mahalalel woke me up, as I was asleep near him. He said, "Why do you cry so, my son, and why do you make such lamentation?"

⁷I told him the whole vision I had seen, and he said to me, "You have

seen a terrible thing, my son, and of grave moment is your dream-vision about the secrets of all the sin of the earth. It must sink into the abyss and be destroyed with a great destruction. ⁸Now, my son, arise and pray to the Lord of glory because you are a believer, that a remnant may remain on the earth, and pray that He may not destroy the whole earth. ⁹My son, all this will come upon the earth from heaven, and upon the earth there will be great destruction."

¹⁰After that, I arose, prayed, implored, earnestly sought, and also wrote down my prayer for the generations of the world, and I will show everything to you, my son Methuselah.

¹¹When I had gone forth below and saw the heaven, and the sun rising in the east, and the moon setting in the west, and a few stars, and the whole earth, and everything as it had been known from the beginning, I blessed the Lord of judgment and extolled Him because He had made the sun to go forth from the windows of the east, and it ascended and rose on the face of the heaven, and kept traversing the same path assigned to it.

CHAPTER 84

I lifted up my hands in righteousness and blessed the Holy and Great One, and spoke with the breath of my mouth, and with the tongue of flesh, which God has made for the children of men with which they should speak. He gave them breath, a tongue, and a mouth with which they should speak,

> ²"Blessed be You, O Lord, King, Great and mighty in
> Your greatness, Lord of the whole creation of the heaven,
> King of kings and God of the whole world. Your power,
> kingship, and greatness remain forever and ever, and
> throughout all generations. Your domain, and all the
> heavens are Your throne forever, and the whole earth
> Your footstool forever and ever.
>
> ³For You made and rule all things, and nothing is too
> hard for You. Wisdom does not depart from the place
> of Your throne, nor turn away from Your presence. You
> know, see, and hear everything, and there is nothing hid-
> den from You. You see everything. ⁴And now the Mes-

sengers of Your heavens are guilty of trespass, and upon the flesh of men remains your wrath until the great day of judgment.

⁵"Now, O God and Lord and Great King, I implore and cry to You to fulfill my prayer to leave me a posterity on earth and not destroy all the flesh of man. Do not make the earth without inhabitant, so that there would be an eternal destruction. ⁶Now, my Lord, destroy from the earth the flesh that has aroused Your wrath. But the flesh of righteousness and uprightness establish as a plant of the eternal seed. Do not hide Your face from the prayer of Your servant, O Lord."

Chapter 85

After this I saw another dream, and I will show the whole dream to you, my son. ²Then Enoch raised his voice and spoke to his son Methuselah. To you, my son, I will speak. Hear my words listen carefully to the dream vision of your father. ³Before I took your mother Edna, I saw a vision on my bed.

Adam and Eve, Cain and Abel

A bull came forth from the earth, and that bull was white. After it came a heifer, and from this came two bulls, one black and the other red.

⁴The black bull gored the red one and pursued him over the earth. And then I could no longer see the red bull. ⁵But the black bull grew and a heifer went with him, and I saw that many oxen proceeded from him that resembled and followed him.

⁶That heifer, the first one, went from the presence of that first bull in order to seek the red bull, but did not find him, and she cried with a great lamentation over him and continued to look for him. ⁷And I looked until I saw that the first bull came to her and quieted her, and from that time onward she cried no more. ⁸After that she bore another white bull, and after him she bore many bulls and black cows.

Seth

⁹I saw in my sleep that that white bull likewise grew and became a great white bull, and from Him proceeded many white bulls, and they looked like him. ¹⁰These began to beget many white bulls, which resembled them, one following the other, even many.

CHAPTER 86

"Angels that sinned"

Again I saw with my eyes as I slept, and I saw the heaven above, and a star fall from heaven. It got up and became a large black ox and began to eat and pasture among the other oxen. ²After that I saw that large and black oxen, and [the other oxen] all changed their stalls, pastures and their cattle, and began to live with each other. ³And again I saw in the vision, and looked towards the heaven, and I saw many stars descend and cast themselves down from heaven to that first star, and they became bulls among those cattle and pastured with them [and lived] among them.

⁴I looked at these [bulls] and saw that they all let out their penises, like horses, and began to have intercourse with the cows of the oxen, and the cows all became pregnant and gave birth to elephants, camels, and asses.

⁵All the oxen feared these [bulls] and were afraid of them. These bulls began to bite with their teeth and devour, and to gore with their horns, ⁶and they began to eat the oxen. All the children of the earth began to tremble and shake with fear before them and to flee from them.

CHAPTER 87

And again I saw how they [all] began to gore each other and eat each other, and the earth began to cry aloud.

²I raised my eyes again to heaven, and in the vision I saw there came from heaven beings that were like white men. Four went from that place, and three others accompanied them. ³Those last three came and grasped me by my hand and took me up, away from the people of the earth, and raised me up to a lofty place, and showed me a tower that stood high above the earth, and all the hills were lower. ⁴And one said to me:

Stay here until you see everything that happens to

those elephants, camels, asses, and to the stars, and to the oxen: all of them.

CHAPTER 88

And I saw one of those four who came first seize the first star that had fallen from the heaven, and bound it hand and foot and threw it into an abyss that was narrow, deep, horrible, and dark.

²Another one of the four pulled out a sword, and gave it to the elephants, camels, and asses. Then they began to war against each other, and the whole earth shook because of them.

³As I was watching the vision, another one of those four, who had come from heaven, stoned the [elephants, camels, and asses] from heaven. Then he gathered and took all the great stars whose penises were like those of horses, and bound them all hand and foot, and threw them in an abyss of the earth.

CHAPTER 89

Noah

And another one of the four went to the white bull and instructed him in a secret, without him becoming terrified.

He was born a bull, but he became a man, and built for himself a great ship and lived on it. Three bulls lived with him in that vessel and they were protected within it.

²Again I raised my eyes towards heaven and saw a lofty roof, with seven violent streams of water on it, and those torrents flowed with much water into an enclosure. ³I looked again and fountains were opened on the surface of that great enclosure, and that water began to swell and rise upon the surface. I watched that enclosure until its entire surface was covered with water. ⁴Water, darkness, and mist increased on it.

As I watched the height of that water, it rose above the height of that enclosure, and streamed over it, and poured upon the earth. ⁵All the cattle of that enclosure were gathered together until I saw how they sank and were swallowed up and perished in that water.

⁶The vessel floated on the water, while all the oxen and the elephants,

camels, and asses sank to the bottom with all the animals, and I could no longer see them. They were not able to escape, and they perished and sank into the depths.

⁷Again I watched the vision until those violent streams of water were removed from that high roof. The chasms of the earth were leveled up and other abysses were opened. ⁸Then the water began to run down into these until the earth became visible. The vessel settled on the earth, and the darkness ended and light appeared.

Shem, Ham and Japheth

⁹Then that white bull, which had become a man, came out of that vessel, and the three bulls with him. One of those three was white like that bull, and one of them was red as blood, and one black. And that white bull left them.

Nations Born

¹⁰And they began to bring forth beasts of the field and birds, so that there arose different genera: including lions, tigers, wolves, dogs, hyenas, wild boars, foxes, squirrels, swine, falcons, vultures, kites, eagles, and ravens; and among them was born a white bull, ¹¹and these began to bite one another.

Abraham

But that white bull, which was born among them, begat a wild ass and a white bull. The wild asses multiplied.

Isaac

¹²But that bull which was born from him begat twins: a black wild boar and a white sheep; and the former begat many boars.

Jacob (Israel)

But that sheep procreated twelve sheep.

The Twelve, Joseph sold

¹³When those twelve sheep had grown, they gave up one of them to

the asses, and those asses again gave up that sheep to the wolves, and that sheep grew up among the wolves. [14]And the Lord brought the eleven sheep to live with it and to pasture with it among the wolves: and they multiplied and became many flocks of sheep.

[15]And the wolves began to fear them, and they oppressed them until they killed their little ones by throwing their young into a river that had much water. Then those sheep began to cry aloud on account of their little ones, and to complain to their Lord.

Moses

[16]One sheep who was saved from the wolves fled and escaped to the wild asses. Then I saw the sheep how they lamented and cried, and besought their Lord with all their might, until the Lord of the sheep descended at the voice of the sheep from a lofty abode, and came to them and pastured them.

[17]He called the sheep that had escaped the wolves, and spoke with it concerning the wolves that it should admonish the wolves not to touch the [flock of] sheep.

Moses, Aaron confront the Egyptians

[18]That sheep went to the wolves according to the word of the Lord, and another sheep met it and went with it, and the two went and entered together into the assembly of the wolves. These two sheep spoke with the wolves and admonished them to never again touch the sheep. [19]But I saw the wolves, and how they exceedingly oppressed the sheep with all their power. And the sheep cried aloud.

[20]The Lord came to the sheep and they began to smite those wolves: and the wolves began to make lamentation; but the sheep became quiet and forthwith ceased to cry out. [21]I saw the sheep until they escaped from among the wolves. But the eyes of the wolves were blinded, and those wolves set out in pursuit of the sheep with all their power.

[22]And the Lord of the sheep went with them, as their leader, and all His sheep followed Him: and his face was dazzling and glorious and terrible to behold.

[23]But the wolves pursued the sheep until they reached a sea of water.

²⁴And that sea was divided, and the water stood on both sides before their face, and their Lord led them and placed Himself between them and the wolves. ²⁵And because those wolves did not see the sheep, they proceeded into the midst of that sea, and followed the sheep, and ran after them into the sea.

²⁶And when they saw the Lord of the sheep, they turned to flee away from His face, but the sea gathered itself together, and became as it had been created, and the water swelled and rose until it covered the wolves. ²⁷I watched until all the wolves that pursued the sheep perished and were drowned.

Deliverance and Sin in the Wilderness

²⁸The sheep escaped from the water and went into a wilderness, where there was no water and no grass; and they began to open their eyes to see. I saw the Lord of the sheep pasturing them and giving them water and grass, and that one sheep going and leading them.

²⁹And the one sheep ascended to the summit of a lofty rock, and the Lord of the sheep sent it back to the other sheep.

³⁰After that I saw the Lord of the sheep, who stood before them. His appearance was great and terrible and majestic, and all those sheep saw Him and were afraid before His face. ³¹And they all feared and trembled because of Him, and they cried to that one sheep with them that was among them, "We are not able to stand before our Lord or to look at Him."

³²That sheep which led them again ascended to the summit of that rock. But the sheep began to be blinded and to wander from the way that he showed them, but that sheep did not know about this. ³³And the Lord of the sheep was exceedingly angry against them, and that sheep discovered it, and went down from the summit of the rock, and came to the sheep, and found the nearly all of them had become blinded and had fallen away.

³⁴When they saw it they feared and trembled at its presence, and desired to return to their folds. ³⁵And that sheep took other sheep with it, and came to those sheep that had fallen away, and began to slay them; and the sheep feared its presence, and as a result, that sheep brought back those sheep that had fallen away, and they returned to their folds.

Tabernacle Built

[36]I watched in this vision until that sheep became a man and built a house for the Lord of the sheep, and placed all the sheep in that house. [37]And I watched until the sheep, which first met the one sheep that led them, fell asleep. So all the great [older] sheep perished and little [young] ones arose in their place. They came to a pasture, and approached a stream of water.

Moses Dies

[38]Then that sheep, their leader that had become a man, withdrew from them and fell asleep, and all the sheep searched for it and cried over it with a great crying. [39]I watched until they stopped crying for that sheep and crossed the stream of water.

Two other sheep arose as leaders in the place of those that had fallen asleep, and they led them.

The Promised Land

[40]I saw the sheep come to a beautiful place, a pleasant and glorious land, and I watched until those sheep were satisfied. And that house stood among them in the pleasant land. [41]But sometimes their eyes were opened, and sometimes blinded, until another sheep arose and led them and brought them all back, and their eyes were opened.

King Saul

[42]And the dogs, foxes, and wild boars began to devour those sheep until the Lord of the sheep raised up another sheep, a ram from their midst, which led them. [43]That ram began to butt on either side those dogs, foxes, and wild boars until he had destroyed them all. [44]And that sheep whose eyes were opened saw that ram, which was among the sheep, until it forsook its glory and began to butt those sheep, and trampled upon them, and behaved itself unseemly.

King David

[45]And the Lord of the sheep sent the lamb to another lamb and raised it to being a ram and leader of the sheep instead of the ram which had

forsaken its glory. ⁴⁶And it went to it and spoke to it alone, and raised it to being a ram, and made it the prince and leader of the sheep; but during all these things the dogs oppressed the sheep.

⁴⁷And the first ram pursued the second ram, and the second ram arose and fled from the first ram; and I watched until the dogs pulled down the first ram.

⁴⁸After that the second ram arose and led the little sheep. ⁴⁹And those sheep grew and multiplied; but all the dogs, foxes, and wild boars feared and fled from the second ram, because that ram butted and killed the wild beasts, and those wild beasts no longer had any power among the sheep and robbed them no more of anything.

King Solomon. Temple Built

And that ram begat many sheep and fell asleep; and a little sheep became ram in its stead, and became prince and leader of those sheep.

⁵⁰And that house became great and broad and was built for those sheep. Also a lofty and great tower was built on the house for the Lord of the sheep. The house was low, but the tower was elevated and high, and the Lord of the sheep stood on that tower, and they offered a full table before Him.

Israel forgets their Deliverer

⁵¹Again I saw those sheep that they again erred and went many ways, and forsook their house.

Prophets Sent

Then the Lord of the sheep called some from among the sheep and sent them to the sheep, but the sheep began to kill them.

Elijah

⁵²One of them was saved and was not slain, and it sped away and cried aloud over the sheep. The sheep sought to slay it, but the Lord of the sheep saved it from the sheep, and brought it up to me and caused it to dwell there. ⁵³And He sent many other sheep to those sheep to testify and witness to them and cry over them.

Israel Lost

⁵⁴And after that I saw that when they forsook the house of the Lord and His tower they fell away entirely, and their eyes were blinded. And I saw how the Lord of the sheep brought much slaughter among them in their herds because those sheep invited that slaughter and betrayed His place. ⁵⁵So He gave them over into the hands of the lions, tigers, wolves, and hyenas, foxes, and to all the wild beasts, and those wild beasts began to tear in pieces those sheep. ⁵⁶I saw that He forsook their house and tower and gave them all into the hand of the lions, to tear and devour them, and into the hand of all the wild beasts.

Unanswered Prayer

⁵⁷And I began to cry aloud with all my power, and to appeal to the Lord of the sheep, and to represent to Him in regard to the sheep that all the wild beasts devoured them. ⁵⁸But He remained unmoved, though He saw it, and rejoiced that they were devoured, swallowed and robbed, and He left them to be devoured in the hand of all the beasts.

Seventy Shepherds Assigned

⁵⁹And He called seventy shepherds, and cast those sheep to them that they might pasture them, and He spoke to the shepherds and their companions:

> Let each individual of you pasture the sheep from this time forward, and everything that I shall command you, that do. ⁶⁰And I will deliver them over to you duly numbered, and tell you which of them are to be destroyed, and these destroy.'

And He turned those sheep over to them.

⁶¹And He called another and spoke to him:

> Observe and mark everything that the shepherds will do to those sheep; for they will destroy more of them than I have commanded them. ⁶²And every excess and the destruction, which will be done through the shepherds, record how many they destroy according to my command, and how many according to their own caprice. Record

against every individual shepherd all the destruction he effects. ⁶³And read out before me by number how many they destroy, and how many they deliver over for destruction, that I may have this as a testimony against them, and know every deed of the shepherds, that I may comprehend and see what they do, whether or not they abide by my command which I have commanded them.

⁶⁴But they shall not know it, and you shall not declare it to them, nor admonish them, but only record against each individual all the destruction which the shepherds effect each in his time and lay it all before me.'

⁶⁵And I watched until those shepherds pastured in their season, and they began to slay and to destroy more than they were bidden, and they delivered those sheep into the hand of the lions.

Temple Burned, Captivity

⁶⁶The lions and tigers ate and devoured the greater part of those sheep, and the wild boars ate along with them; and they burnt that tower and demolished that house. ⁶⁷And I became exceedingly sorrowful over that tower because that house of the sheep was demolished, and afterwards I was not able to see if those sheep entered that house.

⁶⁸And the shepherds and their associates delivered over those sheep to all the wild beasts, to devour them, and each one of them received in his time a definite number. And this was written by the other in a book how many each one of them destroyed of the sheep. ⁶⁹And each one slew and destroyed many more than was [given to each by number]. And I began to weep and lament on account of those sheep.

Records Kept

⁷⁰In the vision I saw the one who wrote, and how he wrote down every one that was destroyed by those shepherds, day by day, and carried up and laid down and showed actually the whole book to the Lord of the sheep. This included everything that they had done, and all that each one of them had made away with, and all that they had given over to destruction. ⁷¹And the book was read before the Lord of the sheep, and He took the book from

his hand and read it and sealed it and laid it down.

⁷²Immediately I saw how the shepherds pastured for twelve hours.

Return from Exile

And three of those sheep turned back and came and entered and began to build up all that had fallen down of that house. But the wild boars tried to hinder them, but they were not able.

Jerusalem and Temple Rebuilt, Unclean Food

⁷²And they began again to build as before, and they reared up that tower, and it was named the high tower; ⁷³and they began again to place a table before the tower, *but all the bread on it was polluted and not pure.*

⁷⁴As touching all this, t*he eyes of those sheep were blinded* so that they did not see. The eyes of their shepherds were also blinded, and they delivered them in large numbers to their shepherds for destruction, and they trampled the sheep with their feet and devoured them.

Israel to be Dispersed Among the Nations

⁷⁵But the Lord of the sheep remained unmoved until *all the sheep were dispersed* over the field and He mingled them with the beasts, and the shepherds did not save them out of the hand of the beasts.

⁷⁶And this one who wrote the book carried it up, and showed it and read it before the Lord of the sheep, and implored Him on their account, and besought Him on their account as he showed Him all the works of the shepherds, and gave testimony before Him against all the shepherds. ⁷⁷And he took the actual book and laid it down beside Him and departed.

CHAPTER 90

And I watched until that in this manner thirty-five shepherds undertook the pasturing of the sheep, and they each in his time completed their periods, as did the first, and others received them into their hands, to pasture them for their period, each shepherd in his own period.

Revolt, War and Dispersion (135 CE)

²After that I saw in my vision all the birds of heaven coming, the eagles,

vultures, kites, and ravens. The eagles led all the birds, and they began to devour the sheep, and pick out their eyes and devour their flesh. ³And the sheep cried out because the birds were devouring their flesh.

As for me I looked and lamented in my sleep over that shepherd who pastured the sheep.

⁴I looked until the dogs, eagles, and kites devoured those sheep, and they left neither flesh nor skin nor sinew remaining on them. Only their bones stood there, and their bones too fell to the earth and the sheep became few.

⁵And I saw until twenty-three had undertaken the pasturing and completed this in their several periods fifty-eight times.

Apostles

⁶But notice: lambs were borne by those white sheep, and they began to open their eyes and to see, and to cry to the sheep. ⁷Yes, they cried to them, but the sheep did not listen to what they said to them, but were exceedingly deaf and their eyes became blinded.

⁸And I saw in the vision how the ravens flew upon those lambs and took one of those lambs, and dashed the sheep in pieces and devoured them. ⁹I saw horns grow upon those lambs, and the ravens threw down their horns.

End Time

[This is the order as in Enoch. Charles shuffles these verses unnecessarily to try to force the prophecy into the past. Ed.]

I watched until there sprouted a great horn on one of those sheep, and their eyes were opened. ¹⁰And that sheep pastured with them, and it cried to the sheep, and the rams saw it and all ran to it.

¹¹But despite all this, those eagles, vultures, ravens, and kites still kept tearing the sheep and swooping down upon them and devouring them, while the sheep remained silent. But the rams lamented and cried out. ¹²And those ravens fought and battled with the sheep with the great horn, and sought to lay low its horn. But they had no power over it.

¹³I watched until the shepherds, eagles, and those vultures and kites came, and they cried to the ravens that they should break the horn of that

ram. They battled and fought with it, and it battled with them and it cried that its help might come.

¹⁴I watched until that man, who wrote down the names of the shepherds, carried up into the presence of the Lord of the sheep.

¹⁵And I watched until the Lord of the sheep came to them in wrath, and all who saw Him fled, and they all fell from among the sheep [and] from before His face.

¹⁶All the eagles, vultures, raven, and kites were gathered together, and there came with them all the sheep of the field. Yes, they all came together, and helped each other to break that horn of the ram.

¹⁷And I saw that man, who wrote the book according to the command of the Lord, until he opened that book concerning the destruction that those last twelve shepherds had wrought, and showed, before the Lord of the sheep, that those shepherds had destroyed much more than their predecessors.

Return of Yahua to the Earth

¹⁸And I saw until the Lord of the sheep came to them and took in His hand the staff of His wrath, and smote the earth, and the earth split apart, and all the beasts and all the birds of the heaven fell away from among those sheep and were swallowed up in the earth, and it covered them.

¹⁹And I saw until a great sword was given to the sheep, and the sheep proceeded against all the beasts of the field to slay them, and all the beasts and the birds of the heaven fled before their face.

Time of Judgment

²⁰And I saw until a throne was set up in the pleasant land, and the Lord of the sheep sat Himself on the throne, and the other man took the sealed books and opened those books before the Lord of the sheep.

²¹And the Lord called those men the seven first white ones, and commanded that they should bring before Him, beginning with the first star which led the way, all the stars whose penises were like those of horses, and they brought them all before Him.

²²And He said to that man who wrote before Him, being one of those seven white ones:

Take those seventy shepherds to whom I delivered the
sheep, and who taking them on their own authority slew
more than I commanded them.'
²³And I saw that they were all bound, and they all stood before Him.
²⁴And the judgment was held first over the stars, and they were judged
and found guilty, and went to the place of condemnation, and were cast
into an abyss, full of fire and flaming, and full of pillars of fire. ²⁵And those
seventy shepherds were judged and found guilty, and they were cast into
that fiery abyss.

²⁶I saw at that time how another abyss was opened in the midst of the
earth, full of fire, and they brought those blinded sheep, and they were all
judged and found guilty and cast into this fiery abyss, and they burned.
This abyss was to the right of that house.

²⁷And I saw those sheep burning and their bones burning.

New Temple (House)

²⁸And I stood up to see until they folded up that old house; and carried
off all the pillars. All the beams and ornaments of the house were at the
same time folded up with it, and they carried it off and laid it in a place in
the south of the land.

²⁹And I saw until the Lord of the sheep brought a new house greater and
loftier than that first, and set it up in the place of the first which had been
folded up. All its pillars and ornaments were new and larger than those of
the first, the old one that He had taken away. And all the sheep were inside
of this new house.

³⁰And I saw all the sheep, which had been left, and all the beasts on
the earth, and all the birds of the heaven, falling down and showing great
respect to those sheep and making petition to and obeying them in every
thing.

All Delivered to Righteousness and Eternal Life

³¹Thereafter those three, who were clothed in white and who had taken
me up before, seized me by my hand, and the hand of that ram also seized
hold of me. They took me up and set me down in the midst of those sheep
before the judgment took place. ³²And those sheep were all white, and

their wool was abundant and clean.

33 ***All that had been destroyed and dispersed, and all the beasts of the field, and all the birds of the heaven, assembled in that house. The Lord of the sheep rejoiced with great joy because all of them were now good and had returned to His house.***

34 And I watched until they laid down that sword, which had been given to the sheep, and they brought it back into the house, and it was sealed before the presence of the Lord. All the sheep were invited into that house, but it could not hold all of them. **35** And the eyes of all of them were opened, and they saw the good, and there was not one among them that did not see.

36 And I saw that that house was large and broad and very full. **37** And I saw that a white bull was born, with large horns and all the beasts of the field and all the birds of the air feared him and made petition to him all the time.

38 ***And I saw until all their generations were transformed, and they all became white bulls; and the first among them became a lamb, and that lamb became a great animal and had great black horns on its head; and the Lord of the sheep rejoiced over it and over all the oxen.***

39 I slept in their midst, and I awoke and saw everything. **40** This is the vision that I saw while I slept, and I awoke and blessed the Lord of righteousness and gave Him glory. **41** Then I wept with a great weeping and my tears stayed not until I could no longer endure it. When I saw, they flowed on account of what I had seen, for everything shall come and be fulfilled. All the deeds of men in their order were shown to me.

42 On that night I remembered the first dream, and because of it I wept and was troubled – because I had seen that vision.

Book of Exhortation and Promised Blessings

🕳️

Some may think this book is simply an after thought or just a collection of scraps. But that is not true. This book consist of more than one document: the very important prophecy of the Weeks, promised blessings on the righteous, an account of the events surrounding the birth of Noah, and "Another Book that Enoch Wrote" in chapter 108.

Interestingly, Enoch wrote most of his books addressed to his son Methuselah. This may not seem unusual in itself, but there is one fact about Methuselah that may not be known. His name means, "when he dies, it will come." This is a reference to the prophesied flood. The same year in which he died, the flood came. He wasn't killed by the flood. He died, then it came. Methuselah died after living 969 years – more years than any other human being, which is the point made in Genesis 5.

He lived through all of Enoch's 300 years of walking with Elohim until Enoch was taken. He also outlived his son Lamech, who was Noah's father. Methusaleh was Enoch's oldest son. Therefore, considering that he lived until the year of the flood, what do you think he did with the books he received from Enoch?

If you said, "Gave them to Noah," I would have to agree.

I did *not* retain Charles' swapping of the positions of chapters 91 and 92. There was also some shuffling of verses from chapters 91 and 93. It mades more sense to move the verses 11-14 in 93 and put them after verse 91:10 as this seems to suit the context nicely. According to Charles', the verses "originally" in 91:11-17 contained the description of the weeks eight and beyond. Maybe someone dropped the parchments. Anyhow, according to

Charles, the division of Enoch into chapters was made "apparently in the sixteenth century."

These changes and mixups reflect a lack of understanding of the theology of Enoch. The shuffling represents an unwarranted attempt to try to make Enoch's theology fit current bias.

This book begins with a summary of prophecies already covered in the other books. These direct our attention to the end of unrighteous rule and the transition to the next age, about which we are about to learn.

Then Chapter 93 presents another list of remarkable prophecies. Enoch describes from, according to his words, books that contain "that which appeared to me in the heavenly vision, and that which I have known through the word of the set-apart Messengers, and have learned from the heavenly tablets." This chapter therefore is a summary of prophecies using a metaphor of "weeks." But don't assume that these represent equal periods of time. Instead, each "week" contains events that provide markers to when these happened. Some "weeks" include prophecies of events that will mark the close of those "weeks."

For our edification the close of the Sixth Week is of great importance. The close of that time is the subject of Daniel's "70 weeks" prophecy and of Olivet prophecies of Matthew 24, Mark 13, and Luke 21. These all work together to create a very accurate picture of the close of the Sixth Week and the conditions leading up to that event.

That leads us into the remarkable prophecies of the Seventh Week, the time in which we live. Because the Sixth Week ended with the dispersion of the Jews in 135 CE, one can see that our age starting at that time has continued now for more than 1,870 years. Therefore, any assumption that Enoch prophesied human existence to last for 6,000 years divided into periods of 1,000 years each is unsupported by Enoch.

The meaning that "a thousand years is as a day, and a day a thousand years" has little or nothing to do with this prophecy. When this is understood we will see that living the "eternal life" takes us out of earth or mass time. *That, which from our point of view, will be, in the context of eternal life, already is!* Therefore there is no slowness in eternal life, as we view life through our impatience.

The prophecies of chapter 93 must be viewed in the context of the second dream of the Book of Dream Visions. They are separate prophecies that present different views of human life, but they agree and confirm each other.

Another concept hidden within this vision of "weeks" is supported by the Feast of Weeks. This is a time between the end of the week that contains the last half of the Feast of Unleavened Bread, and the Feast of Firstfruits. There are "seven complete weeks" that we are to count. Then on the 50th day we celebrate a double High Day – the Feast of Weeks, and the Feast of Firstfruits. Enoch's first Seven Weeks is symbolized by the Seven Complete Weeks mentioned above. This is written about in much detail in my book, "Prophecy Unsealed!"

Finally, Enoch's Weeks must be viewed as *ages of varying length,* and not as "thousand year periods" as some erroneously assume. The prophesied "thousand years" of Revelation is indeed the Eighth Week in this vision. But that does not imply that all Weeks are a thousand years long.

We have been given "seven complete weeks" [*ages*] before life is restored to what was intended, and both heaven and earth are cleaned up.

The remainder of the book returns again to the theology of separating the righteous and the elect from the evil-doers. The world's leaders are stripped of their power, as are the religions. Uncleanness and crookedness is removed from society, and the remainder of the world now looks upon the change, the power, and honor bestowed upon the righteous. This is not meant to show a "supposed" better-than-you, nose tweaking. But rather the beauty of truth, justice, compassion, and love that the righteous held onto during their time living in this oppressive and intolerant world. The righteous now offer prayers and intercede on behalf of their persecutors.

> "But I say to you, love your enemies, bless those curs-
> ing you, do good to those hating you, and pray for those
> who are insulting you and persecuting you, *so that you
> become the sons of your Father in the heavens,* because he
> makes His sun rise on the wicked and on the good, sends

rain on the righteous and on the unrighteous." Matthew
5:44-45 The Scriptures

This is how we must view this distinction between the righteous and the evil-doers and sinners. As noted, all the people of the world will see the righteous, and will then repent and change. Then "all will become white bulls" – the spiritual symbol of cleanliness and purity, and the destiny of humanity created before the universe.

Some may read this and the words of Enoch and conclude that this is 'slavery and an impingement upon our free speech and our rights." But what we experience today is slavery and oppression. The leaders of nations and their priests want to rule over the people, to oppress, steal and destroy. We hear in political rhetoric about how the government must free the people and "spread the wealth." But their kind of freedom has led to increased oppression and poverty. They want bigger government, with large bureau*crazies. And because they know they cannot be trusted, they do not allow room for freedom and trust.* This will come to its appointed end. Then the people will know what real freedom is all about.

> In those days the Lord invited them [the righteous] to
> summon and testify to the children of earth concerning
> their wisdom, "Show it to them, for you are their guides."

Chapters 106 and 107 tell about the events surrounding the birth of Noah. This is interesting and gives a different picture about what life might have been like during that time. This comes to a conclusion with Enoch's words once again telling about his visions and experience:

> And I saw written on the tablets that generation upon
> generation will transgress until a generation of righteous-
> ness arises, and transgression is destroyed and sin passes
> away from the earth, and all manner of good comes upon
> it.

Chapter 108, which starts with "Another Book That Enoch Wrote," *claims* to be written by Enoch for his son Methusaleh, and "for those who will come after him [Methuselah], and *keep the law in the last days.*"

The last phrase is intriguing. Even though some claim to be keeping the law, they are not. Instead, they are trekking on the same path that Israel followed after the nation split and began to ignore the Torah completely and *make things up* as they went along. The House of Israel was removed from the land by the Assyrians, and later the House of Judah was taken away to Babylon. After a couple of generations, the people of Judah came back *led* by the Pharisees who *imposed* a *new* law and calendar.

That "loss of faith" has persisted to this day, and that begs the question posed by this chapter: "Who is keeping the law today?"

Reading on in chapter 108, we find this:

> In this place, which you see here, are cast the spirits of
> sinners and blasphemers, and of those who work wicked-
> ness, and *who pervert everything that the Lord has spoken
> through the mouth of the prophets* including the things
> that will be.

There is something about this short "book" that does not ring true. Enoch, never before mentioned, "the law" in this way, nor did he write about those "who pervert everything that the Lord has spoken through the mouth of the *prophets.*" This reaks of *legal abstraction* making it open to *convenient interpretation,* and thereby dates chapter 108 to post-exilic time.

The theology also does not align with Enoch's writings. There is a tone of bitterness and condemnation in these words that do not match Enoch's more understanding and hope-filled messages.

That this fragment is included in R. H. Charles' translation requires that I retain it here. But between you and me, this does not appear to have been part of the first five books. Instead this sounds very much like the writings of doom and threat from a post-exilic scribe.

That the scribes changed and added to the Scriptures is evident in the Torah, the Prophets, and the Writings. Some edits are helpful, others, such as this chapter are not, and only confuse people to accept the myth that the entire book was written around 200 B.C. But this chapter clearly shows that the *scribes* had a hand in both copying the true writings of Enoch, as well as *giving in to the temptation to add what they thought!*

Note: Keep in mind that "righteous" means "right-doing" or when refer-ring to people or Messengers: "right-doers." Also "wickedness, wicked, sin-ners," refers the practice of "doing wrong" or to those who are "wrong-do-ers."

Book of Exhortation and Promised Blessings

Chapter 91

Now, my son Methuselah, call to me all your brothers and gather together to me all the sons of your mother; For the word calls me, and the spirit is poured out upon me, that I may show you everything that will come on you for ever.

²And Methuselah went and summoned to him all his brothers and assembled his relatives. ³And Enoch spoke to all the children of righteousness and said: 'Hear, you sons of Enoch, all the words of your father, and listen with attention to the voice of my mouth, for I exhort you and say to you, beloved, ⁴love uprightness and walk therein. Do not come near to uprightness with a double heart, and do not associate with those who have a double heart. Walk in righteousness, my sons, and it will guide you on good paths, and righteousness will be your companion. ⁵Because I know that violence must increase on the earth, and a great punishment will be executed on the earth. All unrighteousness will come to an end. Yes, it will be cut off from its roots, and its whole structure will be destroyed.

⁶But unrighteousness will again be consummated [completed] on the earth, and all the deeds of unrighteousness, violence, and transgression will prevail in a twofold degree. ⁷And when sin, unrighteousness, blasphemy, and violence in all kinds of deeds increase, and apostasy, transgression, uncleanness increase, a great punishment will come from heaven upon all these, and the holy Lord will come forth with wrath and chastisement to execute judgment on earth.

⁸In those days violence, unrighteousness, and deceit together will be cut off from their roots, and they will be destroyed from under heaven.

⁹All the idols of the heathen will be abandoned, and the temples burned with fire and removed from the whole earth. And the heathen will be cast into the judgment of fire and will perish in wrath and in grievous judgment forever.

¹⁰And the righteous will arise from their sleep, and *wisdom will arise and be given to them.* ¹¹For who is there, of all the children of men, that is able to hear the voice of the Holy One without being troubled? Who can think His thoughts?

Who is there that can look upon all the works of heaven? [12]And how should there be one who could look into the heaven, and who is there that could understand the things of heaven and see a soul or a spirit and could tell [the difference] between them, or ascend and see all their ends and ponder them or do like them?

[13]Who is there of all men that could know what is the breadth and the length of the earth, and to whom has been shown the measure of all of them? [14]Or is there any one who could discern the length of the heaven and how great is its height, and upon what it is founded, and how great is the number of the stars, and where all the luminaries rest?

[18]And now I tell you, my sons, and show you the paths of righteousness and the paths of violence. Yes, I will show them to you again that you may know what will happen. [19]Now listen to me, my sons, and walk in the paths of righteousness, and do not walk in the paths of violence, because all who walk in the paths of unrighteousness will perish forever.

CHAPTER 92

The book written by Enoch for all my children who shall dwell on the earth, and for the future generations who shall observe uprightness and peace.

[2]Do not let your spirit be troubled on account of the times for the Holy and Great One has appointed days for all things. [3]The righteous one will arise from sleep, and will arise and walk in the paths of righteousness. All his path and conversation will be in eternal goodness and grace. [4]He will be gracious to the righteous and give him eternal uprightness. He will give him power so that he will be endowed with goodness and righteousness, and he will walk in eternal light. [5]Sin will perish in darkness forever and will not be seen from that day forever.

CHAPTER 93

After that Enoch both read and began to tell in great detail from the books. [2]And Enoch said,

"Concerning the children of righteousness and the
elect [chosen] of the world, and concerning the plant of

uprightness, I will speak these things. Yes, I, Enoch, will tell them to you my sons, according to that which appeared to me in the heavenly vision, and that which I have known through the word of the set-apart Messengers and have learned from the heavenly tablets."

³And Enoch began to recount from the books and said,

"I was born the seventh [from Adam] in **the first week**, while judgment and righteousness still endured.

⁴After me there will arise in **the second week** great wickedness, and deceit will have sprung up. And in it there will be the first end. And in it a man shall be saved. After it is ended unrighteousness will grow up, and a law will be made for the sinners.

⁵After that in **the third week** at its close, a man will be set apart as the plant of righteous judgment, and his posterity will become the plant of righteousness for evermore.

⁶And after that in **the fourth week**, at its close, visions of the holy and righteous will be seen, and a law for all generations and an enclosure will be made for them.

⁷After that in **the fifth week**, at its close, the house of glory and dominion will be built forever.

⁸After that in **the sixth week** all who live in it will be blinded, and the hearts of all of them will godlessly forsake wisdom. And in it a man will ascend, and at its close the house of dominion shall be burned with fire, and the whole race of the chosen root shall be dispersed.

⁹After that in **the seventh week** an apostate generation will arise. Its deeds will be many, and all its deeds will be apostate. ¹⁰And at its close will be set apart the elect righteous of the eternal plant of righteousness, to receive sevenfold instruction concerning all His creation.

¹¹After that there will be another [week], **the eighth week**, of righteousness. ¹²And a sword will be given to it

that a righteous judgment may be executed on the op-
pressors, and sinners will be delivered into the hands of
the righteous. ¹³And at its close they shall acquire houses
through their righteousness. And a house will be built for
the Great King in glory forever.

¹⁴After that, in **the ninth week**, the righteous judgment
will be revealed to the whole world, and all the works of
the godless will vanish from all the earth. And the world
will be written down for destruction. And all Mankind
shall look to the path of uprightness.

¹⁵And after this, in seventh part of **the tenth week**,
there will be the great eternal judgment in which He will
execute vengeance among the Messengers.

¹⁶And the first heaven will depart and pass away, and a
new heaven will appear, and all the powers of the heavens
will give seven-times more light.

¹⁷And **after that there will be many weeks without
number forever**, and all will be in goodness and righteousness, and sin will no more be mentioned forever.

CHAPTER 94

And now I say to you, my sons, love righteousness and walk in its paths.
Because the paths of righteousness are worthy of approval and accep-
tance, but the paths of unrighteousness will suddenly be destroyed and
vanish. ²And to certain men of a generation will the paths of violence and
death be revealed, and they will keep themselves far from them [the paths
of righteousness] and will not follow them.

³I say to you, the righteous, do not walk in the paths of wickedness, nor
in the paths of death, and do not draw even get close to them, for fear that
you be destroyed by them. ⁴But seek and choose for yourselves righteousness and a set-apart life, and walk in the paths of peace, and you will live
and prosper.

⁵Hold my words tightly in the thoughts of your hearts, and do not allow
them to be erased from your hearts and allow no manner of temptation
diminish them. Because I know that sinners will tempt men to evilly-treat

wisdom so that no place may be found for her.

⁶Woe to those who build unrighteousness and oppression and lay deceit as a foundation, for they will be suddenly overthrown and have no peace.

⁷Woe to those who build their houses with sin for they will be overthrown from all their foundations, and by the sword shall they fall.

Those who acquire gold and silver in judgment will suddenly perish. ⁸Woe to you who are rich, for you have trusted in your riches, and from your riches you will depart because you have not remembered the Most High in the days of your riches. ⁹You committed blasphemy and unrighteousness, and have become ready for the day of slaughter, and the day of darkness, and the day of the great judgment. ¹⁰I speak and declare to you: He who created you will overthrow you, and for your fall there will be no compassion. Your Creator will rejoice at your destruction. ¹¹And your [so-called] righteous ones in those days will be a reproach even to the sinners and the godless.

CHAPTER 95

Oh that my eyes were a clouds full of rain that I might weep over you, and pour down my tears as a cloud of waters so that I might rest from my trouble of heart!

²Who gave you permission to practice scorn and wickedness? Judgment will overtake you, sinners.

³Do not fear the sinners, you righteous, for the Lord will deliver them into your hands that you may execute judgment on them according to your desires.

⁴Woe to you who send out curses which cannot be reversed; therefore healing will be far from you because of your sins.

⁵Woe to you who repay your neighbor with evil, for you will be repaid according to your works.

⁶Woe to you, lying witnesses, and to those who weigh out injustice, for you will suddenly perish.

⁷Woe to you, sinners, for you persecute the righteous. You will be delivered up and persecuted because of injustice, and its yoke will be heavy upon you.

CHAPTER 96

Be hopeful, you righteous for suddenly will the sinners perish before you, and you will rule over them according to your desires. ²And in the day of the trial of the sinners, your children will mount up and rise as eagles. Your nest will be higher than the vultures. And you will ascend and enter the crevices of the earth and the clefts of the rock forever as rabbits before the unrighteous. The sirens [female demons] will sigh because of you-and weep.

³So do not fear you who have suffered, for healing will be your portion, and a bright light will enlighten you, and you will hear the voice of rest from heaven.

⁴Woe to you sinners, for your riches make you appear like the righteous, but your heart convicts you of being sinners. And this fact will be a testimony against you for a memorial of your evil deeds.

⁵Woe to you who devour the finest of the wheat, and drink wine in large bowls, and tread the lowly under foot with your might.

⁶Woe to you who drink water from every fountain, for suddenly you will be consumed and shrivel up, because you have forsaken the fountain of life.

⁷Woe to you who work unrighteousness, deceit, and blasphemy, because it will be a memorial against you for evil.

⁸Woe to you, you mighty, who with might oppress the righteous, for the day of your destruction is coming. In the day of your judgment many and good days will come to the righteous.

CHAPTER 97

Believe, you righteous, that the sinners will become a shame and perish in the day of unrighteousness.

²Be it known to you sinners that the Most High is mindful of your destruction, and the Messengers of heaven rejoice over your destruction.

³What will you do, you sinners, and where will you flee on that Day of Judgment, when you hear the voice of the prayer of the righteous?

⁴Yes, you shall fare like them against whom this word will be a witness, "You have been companions of sinners."

⁵In those days the prayer of the righteous will reach to the Lord, and

for you the days of your judgment shall come. ⁶All the words of your unrighteousness will be read out before the Great Holy One, and your faces shall be covered with shame. He will reject every work that is grounded on unrighteousness.

⁷Woe to you sinners, who live on the mid ocean and on the dry land, whose remembrance is evil against you.

⁸Woe to you who acquire silver and gold in unrighteousness and say,

"We have become rich with riches and have possessions and have acquired everything we have desired.
⁹Now let us do what we purposed. For we have gathered silver, and many are the farmers in our houses. Our granaries are brim full as with water."

¹⁰Yes and like water your lies shall flow away. For your riches will not remain but speedily go up in smoke from you. For you have acquired it all in unrighteousness, and you will be given over to a great curse.

CHAPTER 98

And now I swear to you, to the wise and to the foolish, for you will have manifold experiences on the earth, ²for men will put on more adornments than a woman, and more colored garments than a virgin. In royalty, grandeur, and power, and in silver, gold, and purple, and in splendor and in food they shall be poured out as water.

³Therefore they will be empty in doctrine and wisdom, and thereby they will perish together with their possessions, and with all their glory and their splendor, and in shame, slaughter, and great destitution. Their spirits will be cast into the furnace of fire.

⁴I have sworn to you, sinners, as a mountain has not become a slave, and a hill does not become the handmaid of a woman, even so sin has not been sent upon the earth, but man of himself has created it, and under a great curse will they fall who commit it.

⁵Barrenness has not been given to the woman, but on account of the deeds of her own hands she dies without children.

⁶I have sworn unto you, sinners, by the Holy Great One, that all your evil deeds are revealed in the heavens, and none of your deeds of oppression are covered and hidden.

⁷Do not think in your spirit nor say in your heart that you do not know and that you do not see that every sin is every day recorded in heaven in the presence of the Most High. ⁸From this time on, you know that all your oppression with which you oppress is written down every day to be kept until the day of your judgment.

⁹Woe to you fools, for through your folly you will perish. You transgress against the wise, and so good fortune will not be your portion. ¹⁰And now, know that you are prepared for the day of destruction, so do not hope to live, you sinners. You will go away and die. For you know no ransom, but instead you are made ready for the day of the great judgment, the day of trial and great shame for your spirits.

¹¹Woe to you, you obstinate of heart, who work wickedness and eat blood. From where did you get good things to eat, drink, and be filled? From all the good things which the Lord the Most High has placed in abundance on the earth; therefore you shall have no peace.

¹²Woe to you who love the deeds of unrighteousness. Why do you hope for good fortune to yourselves? Know that you will be delivered into the hands of the righteous, and they shall cut off your necks and slay you, and have no mercy upon you.

¹³Woe to you who rejoice in the tribulation of the righteous; for no grave shall be dug for you.

¹⁴Woe to you who set at nothing the words of the righteous, for you will have no hope of life.

¹⁵Woe to you who write down lying and godless words, for you write down your lies that men may hear them and act godlessly towards their neighbors. ¹⁶Therefore they shall have no peace but die a sudden death.

CHAPTER 99

Woe to you who work godlessness and glory in lying. Say to them, "You shall perish, and no happy life shall be yours."

²Woe to them who pervert the words of uprightness, and transgress the eternal law, and transform themselves into what they were not made for, into sinners. They will be trodden under foot upon the earth.

³In those days prepare, you righteous, to raise your prayers as a memorial, and place them as a testimony before the Messengers, that they may

place the sin of the sinners for a memorial before the Most High.

⁴In those days the nations will be stirred up, and the families of the nations will arise on the day of destruction.

⁵In those days the destitute will go off and carry their children and abandon them, so that their children will die through them. Yes, they will abandon their children that are still nursing, and not return to them, and shall have no pity on their beloved ones.

⁶And again I swear to you, sinners that sin is prepared for a day of unceasing bloodshed. ⁷They who worship stones, and images of gold, silver, wood, stone, and clay, and those who worship impure spirits and demons, and all kinds of idols not according to knowledge, will get no help from them. ⁸They will become godless by reason of the folly of their hearts, and their eyes will be blinded through the fear of their hearts and through visions in their dreams. ⁹Through these they shall become godless and fearful, for they will have produced all their work in a lie, and will have worshiped a stone. Therefore in an instant they will perish.

¹⁰In those days, blessed are all they who accept the words of wisdom, understand them, observe the paths of the Most High, walk in the path of His righteousness, and become not godless with the godless. For they will be saved.

¹¹Woe to you who spread evil to your neighbors, for you will be slain in Sheol.

¹²Woe to you who make deceitful and false measures, and to them who cause bitterness on the earth, for by this they will be utterly consumed.

¹³Woe to you who build your houses through the grievous toil of others, and all their building materials are the bricks and stones of sin; I tell you, you will have no peace.

¹⁴Woe to them who reject the measure and eternal heritage of their fathers and whose souls follow after idols, for they will have no rest.

¹⁵Woe to them who work unrighteousness and help oppression, and slay their neighbors until the day of the great judgment. ¹⁶For He will throw down your glory, bring affliction on your hearts, and will arouse His fierce indignation and destroy you all with the sword. And all the holy and righteous will remember your sins.

CHAPTER 100

And in those days in one place the fathers together with their sons will be smitten and brothers one with another will fall in death until the streams flow with their blood. ²For a man will not withhold his hand from slaying his sons and his sons' sons, and the sinner will not withhold his hand from his honored brother. From dawn until sunset they will slay one another. ³The horse will walk up to the breast in the blood of sinners, and the chariot will be submerged to its height.

⁴In those days the Messengers will descend into the secret places and gather together into one place all those who brought down sin and the Most High will arise on that day of judgment to execute great judgment among sinners. ⁵Over all the righteous and holy He will appoint guardians from among the holy Messengers to guard them as the apple of an eye, until He makes an end of all wickedness and all sin, and though the righteous sleep a long sleep, they have noting to fear.

⁶And then the children of the earth will see the wise in security, and will understand all the words of this book, and recognize that their riches will not be able to save them in the overthrow of their sins.

⁷Woe to you sinners, on the day of strong anguish, you who afflict the righteous and burn them with fire. You will be payed according to your works.

⁸Woe to you, obstinate of heart, who watch in order to devise wickedness; therefore fear will come upon you, and there will be no one to help you.

⁹Woe to you, sinners, on account of the words of your mouth, and on account of the deeds of your hands which your godlessness as produced, you will burn in blazing flames burning worse than fire.

¹⁰And now, know that from the Messengers in heaven He will inquire as to your deeds, from the sun, from the moon, and from the stars in reference to your sins because upon the earth you execute judgment on the righteous. ¹¹He will summon to testify against you every cloud and mist and dew and rain, for because of you they will all be withheld from descending upon you, and they will be mindful of your sins. ¹²Now give presents to the rain, so that it not be withheld from descending upon you, and to the dew, so that it may descend after it has received gold and silver from you.

¹³When the frost and snow with their chilliness, and all the snowstorms with all their plagues fall upon you, in those days you will not be able to stand before them.

CHAPTER 101

Observe the heaven, you children of heaven, and every work of the Most High, and fear Him and work no evil in His presence. ²If He closes the windows of heaven, and withholds the rain and the dew from descending on the earth on your account, what will you do then? ³And if He sends His anger upon you because of your deeds, you cannot petition Him; for you spoke proud and insolent words against His righteousness. Therefore you will have no peace.

⁴Do you see the sailors of the ships, how their ships are tossed to and fro by the waves, and are shaken by the winds, and are in sore trouble? ⁵Therefore do they not fear because all their expensive possessions go upon the sea with them, and they have convictions in their heart that the sea will swallow them, and they will perish? ⁶Are not the entire sea and all its waters, and all its movements, the work of the Most High? ⁷Has He not set limits to its doings, and confined it throughout the world by the sand? At His reproof it is afraid and dries up, and all fish die and along with all that is in it; but you sinners that are on the earth do not fear Him.

⁸Has He not made the heaven and the earth, and all in it? Who has given understanding and wisdom to everything that moves on the earth and in the sea? ⁹Do not the sailors of the ships fear the sea? Yet sinners fear not the Most High.

CHAPTER 102

In those days when He has brought a grievous fire upon you, where will you flee, and where will you find deliverance? And when He launches His Word against you, will you not be afraid and full of fear? ²All the luminaries will be frightened with great fear. All the earth will be affrighted and tremble and be alarmed. ³All the Messengers will execute their commands, and the children of earth shall tremble and quake and will seek to hide themselves from the presence of the Great Glory; and you sinners will be cursed forever, and you will have no peace.

⁴Fear not, you souls of the righteous, and be hopeful you that have died in righteousness. ⁵Do not grieve if your soul has descended into Sheol in grief, and that in your life your body fared not according to your goodness, but wait for the day of the judgment of sinners and for the day of cursing and chastisement.

⁶Yet when you die, the sinners speak over you saying,

> "As we die, so die the righteous. What benefit do they reap for their deeds? Look, just like us, they die in grief and darkness? So what have they more than we? We are equal. What will they receive and what will they see forever? Behold, they too have died. And from now on forever they will not see light."

⁹I tell you, you doers of wrong, you are content to eat and drink, and rob and sin, and strip men naked, and acquire wealth and see good days. ¹⁰Have you seen the righteous how their end falls out, that no manner of violence is found in them until their death?

¹¹Yet you say, "Nevertheless they perished and became as though they had not been, and their spirits descended into Sheol in tribulation."

CHAPTER 103

Now, therefore, I swear to you, the righteous, by the glory of the Great and Honored and Mighty One in dominion, ²and by His greatness I swear to you. I know a mystery and have read the heavenly tablets, and have seen the holy books, and found written therein and inscribed regarding them [the righteous] ³that all goodness and joy and glory are prepared for them, and written down for the spirits of those who have died in righteousness, and that manifold good shall be given to you in recompense for your labors, and that your lot is abundantly beyond the lot of the living.

⁴The spirits of you who have died in righteousness will live and rejoice, and your spirits will not perish, nor their memorial from before the face of the Great One to all the generations of the world. Therefore no longer fear their harsh language and contempt.

⁵Woe to you sinners, when you have died, if you die in the wealth of your sins, and those who are like you say regarding you,

> "Blessed are the sinners. They have seen all their days.

⁶And how they have died in prosperity and in wealth, and
have not seen tribulation or murder in their life. They
have died in honor, and judgment has not been executed
on them during their life."

⁷Know, that their souls will be made to descend into Sheol and they
shall be wretched in their great tribulation. ⁸And into darkness and chains
and a burning flame where there is grievous judgment will your spirits enter. And the great judgment will be for all the generations of the world.
Woe to you, for you will have no peace. ⁹Do not say in regard to the righteous and good that are in life,

"In our troubled days we toiled laboriously and experienced every trouble, and met with much evil and been
consumed, and have become few and our spirit small.
¹⁰And we have been destroyed and have not found any
to help us even with a word. We have been tortured and
destroyed, and not hoped to see life from day to day. ¹¹We
hoped to be the head and have become the tail. We have
toiled laboriously and had no satisfaction in our work,
and we became the food of the sinners and the unrighteous, and they laid their yoke heavily upon us.

¹²"They that hated us and smote us had dominion over
us. We bowed our necks to those that hated us, but they
pitied us not. ¹³We desired to get away from them that we
might escape and be at rest, but found no place to which
we should flee and be safe from them. ¹⁴We complained
to the rulers in our tribulation, and cried out against those
who devoured us, but they did not attend to our cries and
would not listen to us.

¹⁵But they helped those who robbed us and devoured
us, and those who made us few. They concealed their
oppression, and they did not remove from us the yoke of
those that devoured us and dispersed us and murdered
us. Instead they concealed their murder, and remembered not that they had lifted up their hands against us."

CHAPTER 104

I swear unto you, that in heaven the Messengers remember you for good before the glory of the Great One, [2]and your names are written before the glory of the Great One. Be hopeful; for before you were put to shame through ill and affliction; but now you will shine as the lights of heaven. You will shine, and you will be seen. The doors of heaven will be opened to you. [3]And when your cry, cry for judgment, and it will appear to you, for all your tribulation will be visited on the rulers, and on all who helped those who plundered you. [4]Be hopeful, and do not throw away your hopes for you shall have joy as great as the Messengers of heaven.

[5]What will you be obliged to do? You will not need to hide on the day of the great judgment and you will not be found as sinners, and the eternal judgment will be far from you for all the generations of the world. [6]And now do not fear, you righteous, when you see the sinners growing strong and prospering in their ways. Do not be companions with them, but keep far away from their violence; *for you will become companions of the hosts of heaven.*

[7]Although you sinners say, "All our sins shall not be searched out and be written down," nevertheless they shall write down all your sins every day. [8]And now I show to you that light and darkness, day and night, see all your sins. [9]Do not be godless in your hearts, and do not lie and do not twist the words of uprightness, nor charge with lying the words of the Holy Great One, nor take account of your idols. All your lying and all your godlessness issue not in righteousness but in great sin.

[10]**And now I know this mystery, that sinners will twist and pervert the words of righteousness in many ways, and will speak wicked words, and lie and practice great deceits, and write books concerning *their* words.**

[11]**But when those write down truthfully all my words in their languages, and do not change or take away anything from my words but write them all down truthfully, all that I first testified concerning them, [12]then I know another mystery that books will be given to the righteous and the wise to become a cause of joy and uprightness and much wisdom.**

[13]**To them will the books be given. And they will believe in them and rejoice over them. Then will all the righteous, who have learned from them all the paths of uprightness, be rewarded.**

CHAPTER 105

In those days the Lord invited them to summon and testify to the children of earth concerning their wisdom, "Show it to them, for you are their guides, and a recompense over the whole earth. ²For I and My son will be united with them forever in the paths of uprightness in their lives; and you shall have peace. Rejoice, you children of uprightness. Amen.

CHAPTER 106

And after some days my son Methuselah took a wife for his son Lamech, and she became pregnant by him and gave birth to a son. ²His body was white as snow and red as the blooming of a rose, and the hair of his head and his long locks were white as wool, and his eyes beautiful. And when he opened his eyes, he lighted up the whole house like the sun, and the whole house was very bright. ³And thereupon he arose in the hands of the midwife, opened his mouth, and conversed with the Lord of righteousness.

⁴His father Lamech was afraid of him and fled, and came to his father Methuselah ⁵and said to him,

> "I have begotten a strange son, diverse from and un-
> like man, and resembling the sons of the God of heaven;
> and his nature is different and he is not like us, and his
> eyes are as the rays of the sun, and his countenance is
> glorious.
>
> ⁶"And it seems to me that he is not sprung from me but
> from the Messengers, and I fear that in his days a wonder
> may be wrought on the earth. ⁷Now, my father, I am here
> to petition you and beg you to go to Enoch, our father,
> and learn from him the truth, for his dwelling-place is
> among the Messengers."

⁸When Methuselah heard the words of his son, he came to me to the ends of the earth, for he had heard that 1 was there, and he cried aloud, and I heard his voice and I came to him and said to him, "Look, here I am, my son, why have you come to me?"

⁹And he answered,

> "Because of a great cause of anxiety I come to you,
> and because of a disturbing vision I approached. ¹⁰Hear

me, father. To Lamech my son there has been born a son, the like of whom there is none, and his nature is not like man's nature, and the color of his body is whiter than snow and redder than the bloom of a rose. The hair of his head is whiter than white wool. And his eyes are like the rays of the sun. When he opened his eyes and he lit up the whole house.

[11]Then he stood in the hands of the midwife, opened his mouth and blessed the Lord of heaven. [12]His father Lamech became afraid and ran to me, and did not believe that he was sprung from him, but that he was in the likeness of the Messengers of heaven. So I have come to you that you may make me to know the truth."

[13]And I, Enoch, answered and said to him,

"'The Lord will do a new thing on the earth, and this I have already seen in a vision, and make known to you that in the generation of my father Jared some of the Messengers of heaven transgressed the word of the Lord. [14]They committed sin and transgressed the law, and united themselves with women and committed sin with them, and married some of them, and begot children by them. [15]Yes, there will come a great destruction over the whole earth. There will be a deluge and a great destruction for one year.

[16]And this son who has been born to you will be left on the earth, and his three children will be saved with him. When all mankind that are on the earth will die, he and his sons will be saved.

[17]"And they produced on the earth giants, not according to the spirit, but according to the flesh, and there will be a great punishment on the earth, and the earth will be cleansed from all impurity.

[18]"Now make this known to your son Lamech that he who has been born is in truth his son and call his name Noah, for he will be left to you, and he and his sons will

be saved from the destruction, which will come on the earth on account of all the sin and all the unrighteousness, which will be fully matured on the earth in his days. [19]But after that there will be still more unrighteousness than that which was first consummated on the earth, for I know the mysteries of the holy ones. He, the Lord, has showed me and informed me, and I have read them in the heavenly tablets.

CHAPTER 107

"And I saw written on the tablets that generation upon generation will transgress until a generation of righteousness arises, and transgression is destroyed and sin passes away from the earth, and all manner of good comes upon it. [2]And now, my son, go and make known to your son Lamech that this son, which has been born, is in truth his son, and that this is no lie."

[3]When Methuselah heard the words of his father Enoch, for he had shown him everything in secret, he returned and showed them to Lamech and called the name of that son Noah, for he will comfort the earth after all the destruction.

CHAPTER 108

Another book that Enoch wrote for his son Methuselah and for those who will come after him, and keep the law in the last days. [2]You who have done good will wait for those days until an end is made of those who work evil, and of the might of the transgressors.

[3]And you wait indeed until sin has passed away, for their names will be blotted out of the book of life and out of the holy books, and their seed will be destroyed for ever, and their spirits will be slain, and they will cry and make lamentation in a place that is a chaotic wilderness, and in the fire will they burn; for there is no earth there.

[4]And I saw there something like an invisible cloud; for by reason of its depth I could not look over, and I saw a flame of fire blazing brightly, and things like shining mountains circling and sweeping to and fro. [5]And I

asked one of the holy Messengers, who was with me, and said to him,

"What is this shining thing? For it is not a heaven but only the flame of a blazing fire, and the voice of weeping and crying and lamentation and strong pain."

⁶And he said to me,

"In this place, which you see here, are cast the spirits of sinners and blasphemers, and of those who work wickedness, and who pervert everything that the Lord has spoken through the mouth of the prophets including the things that will be. ⁷For some of them are written and inscribed above in the heaven, in order that the Messengers may read them and know what will befall the sinners, and the spirits of the humble, and of those who have afflicted their bodies, and been recompensed by God.

⁸"Of those who have been put to shame by wicked men, and of those who love God and loved neither gold nor silver nor any of the good things which are in the world, but gave over their bodies to torture. ⁹Who, since they came into being, longed not after earthly food, but regarded everything as a passing breath, and lived accordingly, and the Lord tried them much, and their spirits were found pure so that they should bless His name.

¹⁰"All the blessings destined for them I have recounted in the books. And he has assigned them their reward, because they have been found to be such as loved heaven more than their life in the world, and though they were trodden under foot of wicked men, and experienced abuse and reviling from them and were put to shame, yet they blessed Me.

¹¹"Now I will summon the spirits of the good who belong to the generation of light, and I will transform those who were born in darkness, who in the flesh were not rewarded with such honor as their faithfulness deserved. ¹²And I will bring forth in shining light those who have loved My holy name, and I will seat each on the throne of

his honor.

[13]"And they will be resplendent for times without number; for righteousness is the judgment of God; for to the faithful He will give faithfulness in the habitation of upright paths. [14]They will see those who were born in darkness led into darkness, while the righteous will be resplendent. [15]And the sinners will cry aloud and see them resplendent, and they indeed will go where days and seasons are prescribed for them."

The Witness From Exodus

Although the influence of Enoch can be found throughout the Hebrew Scriptures and the New Testament, the book of Exodus provides some of the strongest evidence that the calendar revealed to Enoch was in force.

The "Revealed" calendar has a set pattern that persists from quarter to quarter and from year to year. The weekly Sabbaths are always on the same days of each quarter and the same days of the year. This means that if we know when a weekly Sabbath occurs on a month, then we can relate that to a position on the Revealed calendar. For example, if we read that a Sabbath is on the 16th day of the month, we know that would be the second month of the quarter.

Some believe that the months of the calendar on which the Feasts and High days fall is a lunar calendar, and the start of the month is a referred to as the "new moon." However, the Hebrew word for "month" חדש (chodesh) is different than the word for "moon" ירח (yareach). The word חדש can be found 276 times in the Hebrew Scriptures. In the King James Version of the Old Testament, it is translated "month" or "new month" 256 times and as "new moon" 20 times; and where it is translated "new moon" it makes more sense to translate it "new month." The true Hebrew phrase for "new moon" *never* appears in the Hebrew Scriptures!

Therefore, the first of each month on the Revealed calendar are חדש and should always be "new month"

JEWISH CALENDAR RULES VS. THE REVEALED CALENDAR

The following calendar rules show a "convenient" compromise that actually breaks the pattern established in the Torah.

Rosh Hashanah postponement rules: Although simple math would calculate 21 patterns for calendar years,

there are other limitations which mean that Rosh Hashanah may only occur on Mondays, Tuesdays, Thursdays,
and Saturdays (the "four gates"), according to the table.

That means that the pattern *can be varied to ensure
that Rosh Hashanah does not fall on the other 3 days.* This
is to *ensure* that Yom Kippur does not directly precede or
follow Shabbat, which would create *practical difficulties*,
and that Hoshana Rabbah is not on a Shabbat, in which
case certain ceremonies would be lost for a year.

Yom Kippur, on which no work can be done, can *never* fall on Friday (the day prior to the Sabbath), to *avoid*
having the previous day's fast day still going on at the start
of Sabbath. Thus some *flexibility* has been built in.

From: http://en.wikipedia.org/wiki/Hebrew_calendar

The tragedy of this "flexibility" is the price Judah and Israel paid for this
"loss of faith." It is as though Eyahuwah (יהוה) could not provide "manna"
or "food" for the Sabbath following the fast of Yom Kippur! But their laws,
received from the Pharisees, caused them to stumble. The Sabbath was a
day of feasting as well as rest. But the prohibitions imposed by a "new law"
made it a burden that the people could not bear!

But, because they were convinced by their teachers that this was the
"law," they put the blame on Eyahuwah and called His Feasts and High
days a burden. In his second dream vision, Enoch saw how the "sheep"
would return from captivity only to get into deeper trouble:

And they began again to build as before, and they
reared up that tower, and it was named the high tower;
and they began again to place a table before the tower,
but all the bread on it was polluted and not pure.
Enoch 89:72-73

Malachi prophesied about this in the Spirit of Eyahuwah:

You are presenting *defiled food* on My altar!
Malachi 1:7 The Scriptures

"But you, you have turned from the way, you have
caused many to stumble in the Torah. You have corrupted
the covenant with Levi," said Eyahuwah of hosts. "And

I also shall make you despised and low before all the
people, because you are not guarding My ways, and are
showing partiality in the Torah."
Malachi 2:8-9

And again, the witness goes against them:

"*From the days of your fathers* you have turned aside
from My laws and did not guard them. Turn back to Me,
and I shall turn back to you," said Eyahuwah of hosts.
Malachi 3:7

Judah has acted treacherously, and an *abomination*
has been done in Israel and in Jerusalem, for *Judah has
profaned what has been set apart to Eyahuwah* – which
He had loved – and has *married* the daughter of a foreign
God! Malachi 2:11

By making a "new law" and by *feasting on polluted bread*, the people of
Israel and Judah cut themselves off from the One who talked face to face
with Moses and entered into a covenant with our fathers, and this continues even to this day in spite of the captivity and the dispersion.

My people do not know the requirements of
Eyahuwah. How then can you say, "We are wise, for we
have the Torah of HaShem," when actually the lying pen
of the scribes has handled it falsely? Jeremiah 8:7-8

EVIDENCE FROM EXODUS: THE TRUE FIRST MONTH

Does what happened during the weeks before and after being delivered from Egypt provide support for the Jewish lunar calendar or for the
Revealed calendar given by the Messenger Uriel to Enoch?

In Exodus 12 Eyahuwah begins to align the people of Israel with the
revealed calendar. First He declares the start of the year:

This month shall be for you the beginning of the
months. ***It shall be for you the first month of the year.***
(12: 2)

Today you are living in the month of ***springtime.*** (13:1)

Then He gives instructions about what is to happen on specific days
during that first month:

On the *10th* day of this month each one is to take for
himself a lamb, according to the house of his father, a
lamb for a household. (vs 3)

And you shall keep it until the *14th* day of the same
month. Then all the assembly of the congregation of Israel
shall *kill* it *between the evenings* [on the 14th]. And they
shall *eat the flesh* on that night [of the 15th], roasted in fire,
with unleavened bread and with bitter herbs they shall
eat it.

Chapter 12 of Exodus focuses on the events of the "sparing." The first
event is the offering of *the sacrifice of sparing* on the fourteenth day. The
sacrifice was made "between the evenings," which some say also means at
"noon." At that time the people were to take the lamb, the *pesach* פסח offering, and kill it on the 14th and place the blood of the lamb on the posts and
lintels of the doors of their homes where they were going to eat the lamb.
Pesach means the "sacrifice of sparing:"

This is *a sacrifice of sparing [pesach]* unto Eyahuwah,
who passed over the houses of the children of Israel in
Egypt when He smote the Egyptians and delivered our
households. Exodus 12:27

Chapter 12 also tells about the seven-day feast that immediately follows. This Feast starts on the *fourteenth* day at its close at sunset, which is
also the beginning of the fifteenth day and continues through the twenty-
first day until its close also at sunset. The Feast begins with the roasting
and eating of the *pesach* on the night of the fifteenth. So the Feast of Unleavened Bread starts on the fifteenth day of the month at sunset. This is
a High Day on which "no servile work is to be done." The twenty-first day
is another High Day on which "no servile work is to be done." The Feast of
Unleavened Bread is seven days long.

On the start of the fifteenth day at sunset, they went into their homes,
roasted the lamb and ate it with unleavened bread and bitter herbs. It is on
this day that the actual "sparing" event happens:

At midnight on the fifteenth Eyahuwah killed all the first-born of Egypt
(vs 29). And Pharaoh "rose up at midnight" as did the rest of Egypt and a
great cry went up. Then he called for Moses and Aaron and told them to

take the Israelites out of the land, as Moses had requested. In the night, Eyahuwah, "passed over" and spared the Israelites, and this moved Pharaoh and the Egyptians to do whatever they could to help the Israelites get out of Egypt immediately.

> And the Egyptians urged [lit: Egypt imposed itself
> strongly upon] the people, to hasten to send them away
> out of the land. For they said, "We are all dying!" And the
> people took their dough before it was leavened, having
> their kneading bowls bound up in their garments on their
> shoulders. (12:33-34)

These are the Feasts and High days of the first month. However, this does not provide sufficient evidence to conclude the days of week for these days.

THE FOOD TEST IN THE WILDERNESS: SECOND MONTH

Chapter 16 provide another fascinating series of events.

> They journeyed from Elim, and the entire assembly
> of the children of Israel arrived at the Wilderness of Sin,
> which is between Elim and Sinai, on the *fifteenth* day of
> the *second* month from their departure from the land of
> Egypt. And all the congregation of the children of Israel
> grumbled against Moses and Aaron in the wilderness.
> (16:1)

The people began to complain against Moses because of food, and the children of Israel said to them,

> "If only we had died by the hand of Eyahuwah in the
> land of Egypt, *when we sat by the pots of meat* and when
> we *ate bread to satisfaction*! For you have brought us out
> into this wilderness to put all this assembly to death with
> hunger."

Upon hearing the complaint Eyahuwah told Moses to tell the people:

> "Look, I shall rain down for you food from heaven. Let
> the people go out and pick each day's portion on its day,
> so that I can test them whether they will follow My Torah
> or not. And it shall be on the sixth day when they prepare

what they bring, it will be double what they pick every day.

I have heard the grumbling of the children of Israel. Tell them, 'At twilight you *will eat meat*, and in the morning *you will be filled with bread*. Then you will know that I am Eyahuwah your Elohim.' "

That evening quail came and covered the camp, and in the morning there was a layer of dew around the camp. When the dew was gone, thin flakes like frost appeared on the desert floor. ... "What is it?" they asked.

Moses told them, "It is the bread Eyahuwah has given you to eat."

Here is the puzzle. The people arrived on the fifteenth day of the month. If this was a Sabbath, then they would have been traveling on a Sabbath. If this was the sixth day of the week, then what? They arrive late on the sixth day with no food and then next day being a Sabbath, known to Moses and Aaron, but not so to the people. So they start to grumble and complain against Moses and Aaron, saying, "What are you trying to do? Starve us to death?"

Moses, however, had a powerful ally, Eyahuwah, who told him to tell the people that Eyahuwah was going to feed them. It doesn't appear that they were impressed, that is, until the cloud appeared in the desert.

'Approach the presence of Eyahuwah, for He has heard your complaints." When Aaron spoke [these words] to the entire assembly of the Children of Israel, they turned to the Wilderness, and behold! – the glory of Eyahuwah appeared in a cloud. 16:9-10

Remember the cloud was with them during the day, and a pillar of fire at night.

Eyahuwah went before them by day in a pillar of cloud to lead them on the way, and by night in a pillar of fire to give them light, so they could travel day and night. He did not remove the pillar of cloud by day and the pillar of fire by night from before the people. Exodus 13: 21:22

So the promise was that they would get meat in the evening and bread in the morning. And it was declared that this would happen every day except on the Sabbath, and they were not to do any gathering (*survival work*) on that Day.

Also, they did not get any food on the day they complained. Instead they had to console their sorry, hungry selves and wait for sunset and see if the food came as promised. And on the evening, the quail came and in the morning the manna.

This continued for six days and on the sixth day, the people gathered twice as much as they did in the previous five days. This was a concern to the leaders who came to Moses and told him what the people had done, because in the first five days, if they gathered too little or too much what each had was the same, no more or no less. But on this day, each went back to his home with twice as before. So Moses told them,

> "This is what Eyahuwah had spoken: *tomorrow is a rest day, a holy Sabbath to Eyahuwah*. Bake what you wish to bake and cook what you wish to cook. And whatever is left over put away for yourselves as a safekeeping until the morning."

Running this back we find that *the sixteenth of the second month had to have been the weekly Sabbath*, which is why the people had to *wait* for the evening and the quail, even though the Sabbath was not something they were in the habit of keeping.

They went to bed on the *fifteenth*, probably tired and hungry after walking all day, then in the morning, they found no food. So the attack rose up against Moses and Aaron, who replied, "What are we, that you should incite complaints against us? ... Your grumbling are not against us, but against Eyahuwah!"

A KINGDOM OF PRIESTS: MONTH THREE

In chapter 19 we learn that in the third month after Israel came had out of Egypt, on the same day of the month, they came to the wilderness of Sinai. Verse 2 shows that they were already camped before the mountain:

> For they set out from Rephidim, and *had come* to the Wilderness of Sinai. And camped in the wilderness. So Israel camped there in the desert in front of the mountain.

The sense is that the distance between Rephidim and the encampment was not very far. And that this chapter starts by showing they had settled into the camped on this day.

Therefore, they were already in place on the *fifteenth day of the third month,* This was to be one of the most significant weeks since the day they walked out of Egypt on the *fifteenth* day of the *first* month.

On this day, Moses went up to Elohim and Eyahuwah called to him and gave him this message to tell to the people:

"You have seen what I did to the Mitsrites, and how
I bore you on eagles' wings and brought you to Myself.
Now, if you diligently obey My voice and shall guard My
covenant, then you shall be My treasured possession
above all the peoples – for all the earth is Mine – and *you
shall be to Me a kingdom of Priests* and *a set-apart [holy]
nation."*

Moses took these words back down and called the leaders of the people and gave them these words as he had been commanded to do. And all the people answered together:

"All that Eyahuwah has spoken we shall do."

So Moses took these words back up the mountain to Eyahuwah. This is one of the shortest and most powerful covenants of the Hebrew Scriptures. Being one of the Chosen people of the earth is looked upon today as a racist and horribly biased statement. But this only shows how far away the people have drifted from their roots. The Nations of Israel (not just the Jews, who come primarily from the one tribe of Judah) have been selected out of all the people on earth as a treasure and to be a Kingdom of Priests, not for themselves, but for all the rest of humanity. The entire creation is waiting for this to become a reality. It is not a mushy sentiment.

The people on earth can be divided into three groups, the righteous (right-doers), the elect (chosen), and the wicked (doers of wrong.) Enoch shows that the righteous will "inherit the earth" and take the thrones from the wicked rulers. The righteous are not part of this world's reality, and are not bamboozled by its religions. The elect consists of both the righteous and those who "shall be to Me a kingdom of Priests and a set-apart nation." Though the elect may not appear to be fulfilling that role now, they "shall"

ENOCH: THE BOOK BEHIND THE BIBLE

in spite of their failures.

Enoch saw the world from a different reality. He saw how the righteous would appear before the people, and that all the others would see them, and then aspire to follow them.

> My *covenant* with him was life and peace, and I gave
> them to him, to fear. And he feared Me, and stood in awe
> of My Name. The Torah of truth was in his mouth and
> unrighteousness was not found on his lips. He walked
> with Me in peace and straightness, and turned many
> away from crookedness. The lips of a Priest should guard
> knowledge, and they seek the Torah from his mouth, for
> he is the messenger of Eyahuwah of Armies. Malachi 2

This is the meaning and significance of the Feast of Firstfruits, the High Day of the fifteenth day of the third month. The very day when this great covenant was made, to which the people of Israel replied:

> *"All that Eyahuwah has spoken, we shall do."*

And so they shall, whether they know it or not. Eyahuwah took them at their word on this day. After the entire nation of Israel is raised from dead as both Enoch, Daniel and Ezekiel saw in their visions, all the Children of Jacob will diligently obey His voice, guard His covenant, and become His treasured possession above all people, and become to Him a kingdom of Priests and a holy nation!

The Appointed Times: Quarter 1

The following calendar, of the first quarter of the year according to the pattern revealed to Enoch, shows the events of the Exodus. Also shown are the other appointed times from Leviticus 23: the Wave Shear (WS) offering, the "Seven Complete Weeks" (W1-W7), the Feast of Firstfruits (FF) that also includes the Wave Loaves offering.

For us, it is difficult to look at this calendar and comprehend that the days start and end at sunset. We have a "burned-in" image of days starting and ending at midnight. So we "interpret" this sunset-to-sunset day and substitute thoughts like, "the Sabbath starts on sunset on Friday." This is unfortunate and leads to confusion. Probably the best way to counter this habit is to view the *vertical lines* between the days as the *sunset lines*, because that is what they are! This takes a little mental agility.

Month one covers the events recorded in Exodus 12 through 15. Month two is Exodus 16 through most of 18; and month three is Exodus 19, which shows the people on the *fifteenth* day camped at the base of Mount Sinai, where they remained for some time.

FIRST MONTH

			1 EQ	2	3	4
5	6	7	8	9	10 LB	11
12	13	14 PS	15 UB	16	17	18
19	20	21 HD	22	23	24	25
26 W1 WS	27	28	29	30		

SECOND MONTH

					1	2
3 W2	4	5	6	7	8	9
10 W3	11	12	13	14	15	16 Fd
17 W4	18	29	20	21	22	23
24 W5	25	26	27	28	29	30

THIRD MONTH

1 W6	2	3	4	5	6	7
8 W7	9	10	11	12	13	14
15 FF WL	16	17	18	19	20	21
22	23	24	25	26	27	28
29	30	31				

KEYS TO THE FIRST QUARTER OF THE CALENDAR
EQ: Spring Equinox. Year Starts
LB: Lambs taken and kept by each household

PS: Passover Pesach (Sparing) Sacrificed

UB: Start of Feast of Unleavened Bread; High Day, Pesach eaten, Israel spared. Passover eaten on the evening of the fifteenth.

HD: High Day , Seventh day of the Feast. Egypt army destroyed.

WS: Wave Sheaf Offering. Seven Week counting begins.

W1 - W7: Seven Complete Weeks. Travel to Mount Sinai.

Fd: The food test begins at sunset after the Sabbath.

FF: Feast of Firstfruits/Feast of Weeks. Wave Loaves (WL) Offered. Kingdom of Priests, Holy Nation covenant confirmed.

THE EVENTS OF THE CRUCIFIXION AND RESURRECTION

It is no accident that the events of the death and resurrection of Eyahushuah (יהושע) also fit within this calendar and its appointed times. The Palm Sunday, Good Friday, and Easter Sunday *pagan-based traditions* are exceedingly poor substitutes for what really happened.

On the *ninth* day of the first month Eyahushuah came to Bethany to the house where Mary, Martha, Lazarus, lived. This is about one half mile from Jerusalem. John 12:1 records that this is six days before the Passover – that is a reference to the actual *sparing* event, which as noted happened on the night of the fifteenth.

The next day – the *tenth* – is the day when the Lamb was picked out and kept. On that day Eyahushuah entered Jerusalem riding on a donkey while the people placed palms leaves on the path. The Lamb was to be kept until the *fourteenth* day and then killed on that between the two evenings or about midday. This day is the third day of the week.

> Therefore, since it was the Preparation Day, that the
> bodies should not remain on the stakes on the Sabbath
> -- for that Sabbath was a High one, the Jews asked Pilate
> to have the legs broken and the bodies taken down. John
> 19:31

After He was killed, His body was taken down and placed in a nearby garden tomb that had never been used. All of these tasks were accomplished in haste

> Because of the Preparation Day of the Jews, they laid

יהושע there because the tomb was near. John 19:42

The Preparation Day was time the people had to clean the leaven out of their homes and get ready for the Passover meal on the night of the fifteenth: a High day and the first day of the Feast of Unleavened Bread.

So, יהושע was placed in the tomb, *before sunset at the end of the fourteenth day!* This was not on Friday, but on the end of the third week day.

יהושע said that the only sign He would give them was that He would be three days and three nights in the tomb and that He would be resurrected **on the third day**. Now refer to the calendar on page 142.

Rather than try to pull magic bunnies out of Easter bonnets and some how fit three days and three nights between Friday and Sunday morning using all the tricks of weird theology, all we need to do is count three days and three nights between the time He was placed in the tomb to find the time when He left the tomb! These must amount to full days and nights, not fractions of days and nights, and that means that if we start with a fraction of a day, we will need to borrow some time on the third day.

We have a very small piece of a day on the 14th; then one night and one day on the 15th, a High Day; one night and one day on the 16th - the fourth weekday; and one night and day on the 17th - the fifth weekday. This brings us to the time just before sunset on the *sixth* day of the week: shortly before the weekly Sabbath on the 18th. This is exactly three nights and three days after he was placed in the tomb. Instead of being raised on Easter Sunday morning, יהושע was up and about on the Sabbath.

Finding the Empty Tomb

There is some controversy over the events that followed His resurrection because of the alternate translations of *mia ton sabbaton*. *Mia* is a form of the word *eis*, which can mean *to, towards, for, another, first, one,* and other things depending on the context. So some translators think that this means "very early on the first [day] of the week." But it could also mean "toward the Sabbath."

Regardless, if the events *post-resurrection* happened on the time just prior to the Sabbath, or early (while still dark) on the first day of the week, nothing changes. This speaks of the time when Mary and the disciples found the tomb empty and that only thing that we can conclude from the passages is that they arrived there *after the fact* of the resurrection.

The weekly Sabbath may have prevented them from arriving on the Sabbath, so they waited until after the first day of the week started at sunset. They may have visited the tomb on both the fifth and sixth days of the week, which were not Sabbath days. But it is not likely that Mary would have taken the burial spices to finish the job just before the Sabbath. Furthermore, the disciples were hiding out! (John 20:19)

The best time might have been after the Sabbath had finished as it was dawning on the first day of the week. But none of this has anything to do with when the resurrection took place. They were not even expecting a resurrection! "They still did not understand from Scripture that יהושע *had to rise from the dead."*

One more event helps put this into perspective.

"But Lord," said Martha, the sister of the dead man [Lazarus], "by this time he stinks, for he has been there *four days!"*

Mary Magdalene was very concerned about this. She knew that they had to place his body in the tomb before the Sabbath High day. No preparations were made. Nicodemus brought myrrh and aloe, but that had not been used. So Mary laid awake most of the night in anticipation of the rising early and running to tomb all the while thinking about how she alone was going to roll back the stone. This was *four and one-half days* since they put him in the tomb! She was also afraid of what she might find – a stinking bloated body! When she arrived and found the tomb open she was on the verge of shock. So she turned and ran back to the disciples.

"*They* have taken the Lord out of the tomb, and we don't know where *they* have put him!"

Peter and another disciple ran back with Mary and examined the empty tomb. Not knowing what to do, the two men returned and Mary remained and cried. She remembered how He was wrapped and placed in the tomb. She knew that more needed to be done.

Then a man approached her, "Woman, why are you crying?"

"They have taken my Lord away," she said, " and I don't know where *they* have put him." She turned an looked him, but did not recognize him.

"Woman, " he said, "why are you crying? Who is it you are looking for?"

Thinking he was the gardener, she said, "Sir, if you have carried him away, tell me where he is, and I will get him."

יהושע said to her, "Mary."

She turned and knew who he was and cried, "Teacher!" and sought to embrace him.

"Do not hold on to me, for *I have not yet returned to the Father*. Go instead to my *brothers* and tell them, ' I am returning to my Father and *your* Father, to my Elohim [the Family name] and *your* Elohim.' "

Mary returned and told the news to disciples.

On the evening of that day, the disciples still in hiding behind locked doors, יהושע came and stood with them and said, "Peace be with you."

What we have not been told remains fixed in the calendar revealed to Enoch and in the Law given to Moses. On the next first day of the week, after the Feast of Unleavened bread was completed, a very special offering was required. This is called the Wave Sheaf offering. This is the offering of the first harvest. A handful of wheat was picked out of the field and presented to Elohim as the first of a great harvest.

יהושע is that Wave Sheaf Offering who returned and ascended to the Father and the Family on the first day of the week after the Feast of Unleavened Bread about eight days after He was raised from the dead.

> Do not be afraid. I am the First and the Last. and the
> Living One. I became dead, and see, I am living forever
> and ever. And I possess the keys of the grave and of death.
> Revelation 1:17-18.

This was a sign of a great event yet to occur when the full harvest takes place and in place of a handful of wheat grass, Wave Loaves prepared from roasted grain with leaven from each household will also be presented before His Father and Their Father, before His Family and Their Family. This also happens *after* they are raised from the dead.

This is the meaning of the Feast of Firstfruits, the fifteenth day of the third month, when a "kingdom of Priests and a set-apart Nation" is revealed to the world. The is seventy-fifth day of year, and, if you understand it, the 1,335th day in Daniel's revelation, which we must aspire to and earnestly wait for!

The Witness From Other Documents

Not only do the Hebrew Scriptures and the New Testament make reference and quote Enoch, other books add even more information about him that enrich our understanding and provide insight into Enoch's time.

This chapter will bring the testimony of the *Book of Jasher*, *The Testiments of the Twelve Patriarchs*, and *The Book of Jubilees*. However, I must caution you to understand that the scribes, as noted, added their falsehoods to these books like they did to the Hebrew Scriptures. The theory of the "inerrancy of Scripture" ignores the history of the Scriptures, and even the rebuke found in the writings of Jeremiah, the prophet, which was also quoted in the prior chapter.

> My people do not know the requirements of
> Eyahuwah. How can you say, "We are wise, for we have
> the Torah of HaShem," when actually the lying pen of the
> scribes has handled it falsely? Jeremiah 8:7-8

"Well," some might moan, "there goes the theory of the 'inerrancy of the Scriptures!'" Because of the intentional changes made by the scribes, it is even more critical that we have the ability to discern the truth with the power of the Spirit:

> "But when the Spirit of truth comes, It will guide you
> into all truth!" John 16:13

This Guide is essential as we delve into documents that have been maligned by both religious leaders and scholars who cannot understand the truth apart from the Spirit.

BOOK OF JASHER

There are two references in the Hebrew Scriptures to a Book of Jasher.

"is it not written in the Book of Jasher?" Joshua 10:13

"Behold, it is written in the Book of Jasher." II Samuel 1:18.

Ok, there they are. In the Book of Jasher, some passages that contain very brief statements are explained in much detail in Jasher and visa versa. Some complaints have been raised by translators that the book, though written in Hebrew, does not contain the vowel points. This should not be a concern. The points were not added until sometime around the ninth century of the current era. Even today Israeli newspapers are printed without the vowel marks unless there is a word or two that is unfamiliar.

The book should not be considered as Scripture in the pure sense. Rather it is an historic document much like books of today about ancient history. Whether the portrayal of events is accurate or exagerated is not something we can decide easily. More than one "witness" is needed to establish the truth in this kind of investigation.

Rather than spending more time on an analysis of the Book of Jasher, which is beyond the scope needed here, my intent is to bring to light in the context of this book information of an historical nature that seems to confirm the context in which Enoch lived.

"I was born the seventh in **the first week**, *while judgment and righteousness still endured.* Enoch 92:3

Here is the story of that "week" or age from the book of Jasher.

THE BOOK OF JASHER, CHAPTER III

Enoch lived sixty-five years and he begat Methuselah; and *Enoch walked with God after having begot Methuselah,* and he served the Lord, and despised the evil ways of men. The soul of Enoch was wrapped up in the instruction of the Lord, in knowledge and in understanding; and he wisely retired from the sons of men, and secreted himself from them for many days.

It was at the expiration of many years, while he was serving the Lord, and praying before him in his house, that a Messenger of the Lord called to him from Heaven, and he said, "Here am I."

The Messenger said, "Rise, go away from your house

and from the place where you hide yourself, and appear to the sons of men, in order that you may teach them the way in which they should go and the work which they must accomplish to enter in the ways of God."

And Enoch rose up according to the word of the Lord, and went from his house, from his place and from the chamber in which he was concealed; and he went to the sons of men and taught them the ways of the Lord, and at that time the sons of men assembled and [he] acquainted them with the instruction of the Lord.

And he ordered it to be proclaimed in all places where the sons of men dwelt, saying, "Where is the man who wishes to know the ways of the Lord and good works? Let him come to Enoch."

And all the sons of men then assembled to him, for all who desired this thing went to Enoch, and Enoch reigned over the sons of men according to the word of the Lord, and they came and bowed to him and they heard his word.

The spirit of God was upon Enoch, and he taught all his men the wisdom of God and His ways, and the sons of men served the Lord all the days of Enoch, and they came to hear his wisdom.

All the kings of the sons of men, both first and last, together with their princes and judges, came to Enoch when they heard of his wisdom, and they bowed down to him, and they also required of Enoch to reign over them, to which he consented. And they assembled in all, one hundred and thirty kings and princes, and they made Enoch king over them and they were all under his power and command. And Enoch taught them wisdom, knowledge, and the ways of the Lord; and he made peace amongst them, and peace was throughout the earth during the life of Enoch.

Enoch reigned over the sons of men two hundred and

forty-three years. He did justice and righteousness with all his people, and he led them in the ways of the Lord.

These are the generations of Enoch, Methuselah, Elisha, and Elimelech, three sons; and their sisters were Melca and Nahmah, and Methuselah lived eighty-seven years and he begat Lamech.

It was in the fifty-sixth year of the life of Lamech when Adam died; nine hundred and thirty years old was he at his death, and his two sons, with Enoch and Methuselah his son, buried him with great pomp, as at the burial of kings, in the cave which God had told him.

In that place all the sons of men made a great mourning and weeping on account of Adam; it has therefore become a custom among the sons of men to this day. Adam died because he ate of the tree of knowledge; he and his children after him, as the Lord God had spoken.

It was in the year of Adam's death which was the two hundred and forty-third year of the reign of Enoch, in that time Enoch resolved to separate himself from the sons of men and to secret himself as at first in order to serve the Lord. And Enoch did so, but did not entirely secret himself from them, but kept away from the sons of men three days and then went to them for one day.

During the three days that he was in his chamber, he prayed to, and praised the Lord his God, and the day on which he went and appeared to his subjects he taught them the ways of the Lord, and all they asked him about the Lord he told them.

He did in this manner for many years, and he afterward concealed himself for six days, and appeared to his people one day in seven; and after that once in a month, and then once in a year, until all the kings, princes and sons of men sought for him, and desired again to see the face of Enoch, and to hear his word; but they could not, as all the sons of men were greatly afraid of Enoch, and they feared to approach him on account of the Godlike awe that was seated upon his countenance; therefore no man could look at him, fearing he might be punished and die.

All the kings and princes resolved to assemble the sons of men, and to come to Enoch, thinking that they might all speak to him at the time when he should come forth amongst them, and they did so.

And the day came when Enoch went forth and they all assembled and came to him, and Enoch spoke to them the words of the Lord and he taught them wisdom and knowledge, and they bowed down before him and they said, "May the king live! May the king live!"

Some time after, when the kings and princes and the sons of men were speaking to Enoch, and Enoch was teaching them the ways of God, a Messenger of the Lord called to Enoch from heaven, and wished to bring him up to heaven to make him reign there over the sons of God, as he had reigned over the sons of men upon earth.

When Enoch heard this he went and assembled all the inhabitants of the earth, and taught them wisdom and knowledge and gave them divine instructions, and he said to them, "I have been required to ascend into heaven, I therefore do not know the day of my going. Now therefore I will teach you wisdom and knowledge and will give you instruction before I leave you, how to act upon earth whereby you may live."

And he taught them wisdom and knowledge, and gave them instruction, and he reproved them, and he placed before them statutes and judgments to do upon earth, and he made peace among them, and he taught them everlasting life, and dwelt with them some time teaching them all these things.

At that time, when the sons of men were with Enoch and Enoch was speaking to them, they lifted up their eyes and the likeness of a great horse descended from heaven, and the horse paced in the air;

They told Enoch what they had seen, and Enoch said to them, "On my account does this horse descend upon earth; the time is come when I must go from you and I shall no more be seen by you." And the horse descended at that time and stood before Enoch, and all the sons of men that were with Enoch saw him.

And Enoch then again ordered a message to be proclaimed, "Where is the man who delighteth to know the ways of the Lord his God? Let him come this day to Enoch before he is taken from us."

And all the sons of men assembled and came to Enoch that day; and all the kings of the earth with their princes and counsellors remained with him that day; and Enoch then taught the sons of men wisdom and knowledge, and gave them divine instruction; and he bade them serve the Lord and walk in his ways all the days of their lives, and he continued to make peace amongst them.

After this he rose up and rode upon the horse; and he went forth and all the sons of men went after him, about eight hundred thousand men; and they went with him one day's journey.

The second day he said to them, "Return home to your tents. Why will you go? Perhaps you may die!" And some of them went from him, but those that remained went with him six day's journey; and Enoch said to them every day, "Return to your tents, lest you may die." But they were not willing to return, and they went with him.

On the sixth day some of the men remained and clung to him and said to him, "We will go with you to the place where you go. As the Lord lives, only death shall separate us." And they urged so much to go with him, that he ceased speaking to them, but they went after him and would not return;

When the kings returned they caused a census to be taken, in order to know the number of remaining men that went with Enoch; and it was on the seventh day that Enoch ascended into heaven in a whirlwind, with horses and chariots of fire.

On the eighth day all the kings that had been with Enoch sent to bring back the number of men that were with Enoch, in that place from which he ascended into heaven. And all those kings went to the place and they found the earth there filled with snow, and upon the snow were large stones of snow, and one said to the other, "Come, let us break through the snow and see, perhaps the men that remained with Enoch are dead, and are now under the stones of snow." and they searched but could not find him, for he had ascended into heaven.

CHAPTER IV

All the days that Enoch lived upon earth, were three hundred and sixty-five years.

After Enoch had ascended into heaven, all the kings of the earth rose and took Methuselah his son and anointed him, and they caused him to reign over them in the place of his father.

Methuselah acted uprightly in the sight of God, as his father Enoch had taught him, and he likewise during the whole of his life taught the sons of men wisdom, knowledge and the fear of God, and he did not turn from the good way either to the right or to the left.

But in the latter days of Methuselah, the sons of men turned from the Lord, they corrupted the earth, they robbed and plundered each other, and they rebelled against God and they transgressed, and they corrupted their ways, and would not hearken to the voice of Methuselah, but rebelled against him. And the Lord was exceedingly wroth against them.

The Book of Jasher continues with the story of Noah and Methusaleh trying to teach the people of the earth in the same manner as Enoch, but the people refused to listen. The world became more corrupt as Mankind began to learn from the Watchers things of unrighteousness, war, and crookedness.

> After me there will arise in **the second week** great
> wickedness, and deceit will have sprung up. And in it
> there will be the first end. And in it a man shall be saved.
> After it is ended unrighteousness will grow up, and a law
> will be made for the sinners. Enoch 92:4

What is only a few words in Genesis, is explained in much more detail in the Book of Jasher. As I wrote in my blog and other books, the Bible raises more questions than it answers. These documents provide much more insight into Enoch's day.

THE TESTAMENTS OF THE TWELVE PATRIARCHS

This book contains the last words of the sons of Jacob to their offspring. There are many insights provided by their words that explain many of the questions not answered in the Bible.

For example, the sins of the Judah's sons, referred to a "Onan's sin," had little or nothing to do with sexual practices. Instead, the mother, Judah's wife, did not want her son's to conceive children with Tamar, but with a woman from her own tribe that was not descendant from the line of Shem through Abraham!

The following segments taken from R. H. Charles translation are only those passages where the Enoch is either quoted or mentioned.

Reuben

> Flee, therefore, fornication, my children, and com-
> mand your wives and your daughters, that they adorn not
> their heads and faces *to deceive the mind*: because every
> woman who uses these wiles has been reserved for eter-
> nal punishment. For in this way, they allured the Watch-
> ers who were before the flood; for as these continually be-
> held them, they lusted after them, and they conceived the
> act in their mind; for they changed themselves into the

shape of men, and *appeared to them when they were with their husbands.* And the women *lusting in their minds* after their forms, gave birth to giants, for the Watchers *appeared to them as reaching even unto heaven.*

Simeon

For I have seen it inscribed *in the writing of Enoch* that your sons shall be corrupted in fornication, and shall do harm to the sons of Levi with the sword. But they shall not be able to withstand Levi; for he shall wage the war of the Lord, and shall conquer all your hosts. And they shall be few in number, divided in Levi and Judah, and there shall be none of you for sovereignty, even as also our father prophesied in his blessings.

Levi

Now, therefore, observe whatsoever I command you, children: for whatsoever things *I have heard from my fathers I have declared unto you.* And behold I am clear from your ungodliness and transgression, which you shall commit *in the end of the ages* [Sixth Week], deceiving Israel, and stirring up against it great evils from the Lord. And you shall deal lawlessly together with Israel, so He shall not bear with Jerusalem because of your wickedness; but the veil of the temple shall be rent, so as not to cover your shame. And you shall be scattered as captives among the Gentiles, and shall be for a reproach and for a curse there. For the house which the Lord shall choose shall be called Jerusalem [Foundation of Peace], *as is contained in the book of Enoch the righteous.*

Dan

Observe, therefore, my children, the commandments of the Lord, and keep His law; Depart from wrath, and hate lying, That the Lord may dwell among you, And Beliar may flee from you. Speak truth each one with his neighbour. So shall you not fall into wrath and confusion; But you shall be in peace, having the God of peace, So shall no war prevail over you. Love the Lord through all your life, and one another with a true heart.

I know that in the last days ye shall depart from the Lord, And you shall provoke Levi unto anger, And fight against Judah; But you shall not prevail against them, For an angel of the Lord shall guide them both; For by them shall Israel stand. And whensoever you depart from the Lord, you shall walk in all evil and work the abominations of the Gentiles, going a-whoring after women of the lawless ones, while with all wickedness the spirits of wickedness work in you. [*For I have read in the book of Enoch, the righteous, that your prince is Satan, and that all the spirits of wickedness and pride will conspire to attend constantly on the sons of Levi, to cause them to sin before the Lord.* And my sons will draw near to Levi. And sin with them in all things; And the sons of Judah will be covetous, plundering other men's goods like lions.] Therefore shall you be led away [with them] into captivity, and there shall you receive all the plagues of Egypt and all the evils of the Gentiles. And so when you return to the Lord you shall obtain mercy, and He shall bring you into His sanctuary, And He shall give you peace. And there shall arise unto you from the tribe of [Judah and of] Levi the salvation of the Lord; And he shall make war against Beliar. And execute an everlasting vengeance on our enemies.

Napthali

Be you, therefore, not eager to corrupt your doings through covetousness or with vain words to beguile your souls; because if you keep silence in purity of heart, you shall understand how to hold fast the will of God, and to cast away the will of Beliar. Sun and moon and stars change not their order; so do you also not change the law of God in the disorderliness of your doings. The Gentiles went astray, and forsook the Lord, and changed their order, and obeyed stocks and stones, spirits of deceit.

But you shall not be so, my children, recognizing in the firmament, in the earth, and in the sea, and in all created things, the Lord who made all things, that you become not as Sodom, which changed the order of nature. *In like manner the Watchers also changed the order of their nature, whom the Lord cursed at the flood, on whose account He made the earth without inhabitants and fruitless.*

These things I say to you, my children, *for I have read in the writing of Enoch that you yourselves also shall depart from the Lord,* walking according to all the lawlessness of the Gentiles, and you shall do according to all the wickedness of Sodom. And the Lord shall bring captivity upon you, and there shall you serve your enemies, and you shall be bowed down with every affliction and tribulation, until the Lord has consumed you all. And after you have become minished and made few, you shall return and acknowledge the Lord your God; and He shall bring you back into your land, according to His abundant mercy. And it shall be, that after that they come into the land of their fathers, they shall again forget the Lord and become ungodly. And the Lord shall scatter them upon the face of all the earth, until the compassion of the Lord shall come, a man working righteousness and working mercy unto all them that are afar off, and to them that are near.

Benjamin

And I believe that there will be also evil-doings among you, from the words of Enoch the righteous: that ye shall commit fornication with the fornication of Sodom, and shall perish, all save a few, and shall renew wanton deeds with women; and the kingdom of the Lord shall not be among, you, for straightway He shall take it away. Nevertheless the temple of God shall be in your portion, and the last (temple) shall be more glorious than the first. And the twelve tribes shall be gathered together there, and all the Gentiles, until the Most High shall send forth His salvation in the visitation of an only begotten prophet.

For all these things they gave us for an inheritance, saying: Keep the commandments of God, until the Lord shall reveal His salvation to all Gentiles. *And then shall you see Enoch, Noah, and Shem, and Abraham, and Isaac, and Jacob, rising on the right hand in gladness. Then shall we also rise, each one over our tribe, worshipping the King of heaven. Then also all men shall rise, some unto glory and some unto shame. And the Lord shall judge Israel first, for their unrighteousness;* And then shall He judge all the Gentiles, and He shall convict Israel through the chosen ones of the Gentiles, even as He reproved Esau through the Midianites, who deceived their brethren, becoming therefore children in the portion of them that fear the Lord. If you therefore, my children, walk in holiness according to the commandments of the Lord, you shall again dwell securely with me, and *all Israel* shall be gathered unto the Lord.

In the above segment, I removed the additional text made by an overzealous Christian scribe, which were out of context here.

THE BOOK OF JUBILEES (יובל)

The Hebrew word translated Jubilee or Jubile (KJV) means *trumpet* or *ram's horn*. The blowing of the trumpet on the forty-ninth year on the tenth day of the seventh month signaled a time of liberty and restoration to come in the fiftieth year:

You shall number seven sabbaths (weeks) of years to you, seven times seven years; and the space of the seven sabbaths (weeks) of years shall be to you *forty-nine* years. *Then you shall cause the trumpet of the Jubilee to sound on the tenth day of the seventh month, in the day of atonement (YOM KPR) shall you make the trumpet sound throughout all your land.*

And you shall *hallow the fiftieth* year, and **proclaim liberty throughout all the land unto all the inhabitants**

thereof: it shall be a jubilee unto you; and you shall return
every man to his possession, and you shall return every
man to his family.

A jubilee shall that fiftieth year be to you. You shall
not sow, neither reap that which grows of itself in it, nor
gather the grapes in it of your vine undressed. For it is the
jubilee; it shall be holy [set-apart] to you: you shall eat the
increase thereof out of the field.
From Leviticus 25

The Jubilee year starts on the first day of the first month of the calendar revealed to Enoch. That is also the spring equinox. Did you catch the
phrase used on the Liberty Bell?

The following are examples of how the Jubilee years played out in the
life of nations and people, *when the conditions are right.*
"Enoch walked with Elohim 300 years" or six Jubilees, then Elohim
took him away. This started when he was 65 years old.

For the history of Enoch is made a testimony (witness)
to the generations of eternity to announce all the deeds of
the generation on the day of judgment. Jubilees 10:15
On July 4, 1826 Thomas Jefferson died. A few hours later on the same
day John Adams also died. Adams claimed he would "outlive Jefferson."
These two were the architects of the Declaration of Independence *that
gave birth to this new Nation, The United States of America.* The day of their
deaths was "50 years to the day from the birth of the country they founded." The start of the United States was therefore signified by a Jubilee.

The "Book of Jubiless" is a record of events that happened on Jubilee
years. Although this book looks at sequential Jubilee years, there is no reason to conclude that every significant event has to fall in line with this se-
quence of Jubilee years. But in history, where spiritual forces are working
in the lives of people, Jubilee years are not uncommon.

A Jubilee Year is the next year after seven seven-year
periods (49 years), and is the 50th year. It is a "hallowed"
or set-apart year. The counting of Jubilees starts when

some new spiritual event happens like the start of a new set-apart nation, or a person is set-apart by receiving the set-apart (holy) Spirit.

CONCERNING THE BOOK OF JUBILEES

The author of the book is unknown. It bears the marks of being tampared with by both the scribes and by the English translators. The hallmark of the book is the use of the Enoch's revealed calendar, which apparently was to counter the use of the Babylonian lunar calendar that had been adopted, contrary to the Law, to become the Jewish calendar. In the book are also a couple of messianic, prophecy passages, but not as much as in the Book of Enoch.

The only complete version of Jubilees is in Ethiopian, although large fragments in Greek, Latin and Syriac are also known. Some believe that it was originally written in Hebrew. R.H. Charles, the translator, concluded that Jubilees was a version of the Pentateuch, written in Hebrew. Interestingly, parts of book became incorporated into the earliest Greek translation of the Hebrew Scriptures called the Septuagint.

The author of the Book of Jubiliees, convinced that the lunar calendar system with its natural 19-year cycle produced serious and bad effects when used for religious practice. This view is shared by the prophets of the Hebrew Scriptures as a cause of the captivities and a prophecy of the coming dispersion of the people. The proper observance of the feasts, which had been prescribed by divine authority, is rendered impossible so long as the right principles for regulating the calendar are ignored. These principles are justified from the written Law, and are represented as having been ordained in heaven.

To what party or tendency in Judaism did the author belong? It is very difficult to believe, as Dr. Charles contends, that the author was a Pharisee, for the positions he advocates are in many respects fundamentally opposed to Pharisaic practice. In particular, how can any member of the Pharisaic party, which from its beginning championed popular religious custom, have advocated a solar calendar?

"New Moon?"

Like all of Scripture, scribes from before the two kingdoms of Israel went into captivity and afterward, made changes to the text that were false. And they were not alone. They had some help from the translators.

The phrase "at the new moon of the first month, and in the new moon of the fourth month and in the new moon of the seventh month, and in the new moon of the tenth month" and so on in chapter VI, is a scribal or translator entry that is just wrong and inconsistent with the context of even that chapter.

For example, starting in verse 34 of that same chapter is written

> And there will be those who will make observations
> of the moon, for this one (the moon) *corrupts* the stated
> times and comes out earlier each year by ten days [a ref-
> erence to the Book of Enoch] And in this way they will
> corrupt the years and will observe *a wrong day* as the day
> of testimony and a corrupted festival day, and everyone
> will mix holy days with unclean ones and unclean with
> holy; for they will err as to months and sabbaths and festi-
> vals and jubilees.

Then immediately following this the scribe or translator jumps back in to try to make a liar out of the original writer.

In every place where "new moon" is found it should have been trans-lated this way:

> At the *first day* of the first month, and in the *first day*
> of the fourth month, and in the *first day* of the seventh
> month, and in the *first day* of the tenth month ...

If we learned anything from Enoch, we should recognize these days as the vernal equinox, the summer solstice, the autumnal equinox, and the winter solstice – the days that signify the beginning of each quarter in the calendar revealed to Enoch by Uriel! These are also the days from which the Festivals and High Days are determined. The "moon" is a corrupting influence and must be ignored.

> A great sign was seen in the heaven: a woman [Israel]
> clad with the sun [the revealed solar calendar,] with the
> moon under her feet [subordinated], and on her head a

crown of twelve stars [one unique star for each month].
Revelation 12:1

Epilogue

T o have a part in bringing our father Enoch's words to those who will truly benefit from them has been an honor and a privelege. Enoch had what I have called, the Elahim or Elohim Connection. He walked with and was one with the Elohim, received knowledge found only in the libraries of that heavenly domain, dealt face-to-face with both the righteous Messengers and with those Messengers that sinned, and was a faithful witness to what he saw and learned.

All that he wrote and preserved he intended to be received by all his posterity, and in particular, those now living at the end of the Seventh Week.

The visions of Enoch are often misunderstood. For example, he saw the time, still in our future, when the earth will be ruled only by the righteous, and today, there are those who consider that to be "poliltically incorrect." They consider that concept to be an abridgement of "religious freedom." But the opposite is true. The future promises freedom *from* religious tryanny, and from politically motivated oppression.

The presence of the right-doers in plain view of the rest of humanity will prove once and forever what true Life is. Enoch shows how the people will marvel at what they observe and experience, and will repent and change their ways so they can be part of the high esteem given to the righteous.

We have been given a choice. We can divorce ourselves from the ways of the world now and begin walking with the Elohim as our father Enoch did. This requires wisdom, knowledge and understanding be given to each of us, along with the gift of seeing all things through the Spirit from Elohim – that is, seeing what They see and understanding Life as They do.

This Spiritual Connection opens the way to becoming "clothed with white robes" of righteousness and becoming the purified Children of Elah.

Nothing can change lives more dramatically than becoming *one of the insiders* to this powerful Spiritual Kingdom.

The greater blessings come to those who walk this Path *now*. Later, the rest will surely, according to the *inside information* given to Enoch, be on the outside looking in and longing to be a participant.

This is not some pie-in-the-sky fantasy. Nor is it a Pollyanna view of life in this world. If you can comprehend the Spiritual message that Enoch was allowed to see, read, understand, and write for us, you will be filled with hope and joy that transcends any *good* this world has to offer.

Only those who know this Secret can bring Light and Life to those with whom we share this planet. That requires shedding our life of "independence" and instead live the life of Oneness with our Family.

Jesus (Eyahushuah) told his students, "I am the Way, the Truth, and the Life." Was this reserved *only* for him, and that made him *special*? Enoch shows that we will be righteous as he is, we will know the Truth, and walk the same Path, and live the same Life as he, the Son of Man, did.

If he became a Son of God, then so will we. If his Father was the One, Elah, then so is ours. If he was raised from the dead and presented before his Father as the *"first"* (the Wave Sheaf), then so will we share that experience (the Wave Loaves) on the Feast of *Firstfruits*. If his family is the Family of Elah (the Elohim), then so is ours.

Now is our time to present ourselves to the world, not as wimpy followers of insipid religions, but as examples of the Way, the Truth, and the Life. The religions teach us to think of the Father, not as a *Father*, but as a nice *sentiment*. They avoid the Reality that the future of humankind, understood by our father Enoch, is Life in the Family, where Elah is our Father, the Spirit our Mother, and the Son of Man our Brother.

Read, study, memorize, and learn the words of your father Enoch. He wrote the future of our Life – yours and mine – as intended before the universe existed, and it is *high noon* – time to come out of darkness and into the Light. We now live in a world gone mad It is *our* time to walk with Elah and bring Light to this world.

Following in the footsteps of Moses, the prophets, apostles and other men of God, we will recognize that Enoch, indeed wrote "The Book Behind the Bible."